REVIEWS FOR

Gaudy Baubles and Fartworms

Terry Smith has spent twenty-six years serving the citizenry, and in this book, he tells it like it is from inside that service. Drawing from decades of compassionate, efficient and effective service, he provides relevant insight and suggestions on how to support and uplift people through the system.

He walks us through the history of welfare, from its original beginnings to where it is today, as well as the challenges/bumps it has undergone through the years. He also points out its shortcomings in meeting its mission. If you want to know how a program works, listen to the people implementing it at the grassroots level, and not just to individuals who think they know what is best for the people.

—Nancy Stiles, former New Hampshire State Senator

This book provides a rare opportunity to hear a candid presentation from one of the most skilled administrators in the field of public welfare. Public welfare programs are implanted in a political system which you will see leads to a multiplicity of problems, as does the long standing stigma attached to those receiving welfare, particularly those receiving food stamps who suffer from poverty including some with mental illness. My best advice - read the book. You will not be bored.

—Jim MacKay, PhD, MSW, active New Hampshire State Representative and Former chairman and current member, NH House Committee on Health, Human Services and Elderly Affairs.

The reality is that elected officials don't know as much as the professionals hired to, well, be the professional—the subject matter expert. When the elected officials don't listen to them, money is wasted, and more importantly, our children don't get a chance at the future they deserve and that we need them to have so they can be the educated workforce and parent the next generation to success. Terry Smith's book provides a history of the welfare system and the landmarks where we went wrong in New Hampshire and in the country. It should be required reading for those legislators who are serving on health and human service committees and commissions. The system is complicated but if our elected officials put down the gaudy baubles and work hand in hand with the professionals hired to do the job, we can create a system that works for our children, for their parents and for the taxpayers.

—Martha McLeod, former New Hampshire State Representative and Vice-Chair, NH House Committee on Finance, Division III

Terry Smith is an expert in the field of Health & Human Services and many of the programs established to help individuals and families experiencing hardship. The programs offered through various Federal and State programs are part of the safety net for those most vulnerable in our society. This population includes both adults and children at risk of homelessness and food insecurity. Gaudy Baubles and Fartworms challenges the status quo and identifies some of the ridiculous political policies and inefficiencies in delivering those programs. This systemic issue keeps people stuck in the very programs meant to raise them out of poverty. Policy-makers and the public should read this book to become more aware of the need to fix these programs and recognize that Fartworms are not necessarily the ones to fix it.

—Robert Mack, Municipal Welfare Officer and former President of the New Hampshire Local Welfare Administrators Association

Having worked on the Quality Control side of public assistance programs for more than thirty years I developed a crust of cynicism. Mr. Smith's detailing of the fraudulent gaming of the Food Stamp Program is on target. This is by far the most outrageous fraud I witnessed in a long career. And Terry Smith may be understating it. The factors that allowed this to be spawned were and are the arcane complexities of the program, the political pressures for state program managers to show acceptable performance and the status of getting financial bonus awards. Probably more than a couple of the "Osnes states" had state human services commissioners on contract without an inkling of what was going on in their state. When these human services CEO's eventually caught on it was too late. Imagine how difficult it would be to change course after achieving the acclaim, financial award, and recognition of being a "high performing" state. Furthermore, all this is in a political envi-ronment at both the state and federal level.

If the states were compromised, the USDA Food and Nutrition Service was similarly compromised and was in so deep there seemed no way out. Certainly some FNS [USDA Food and Nutrition Service] professionals breathed a sigh of relief that they had moved on to a new job or retired before the scandal hit. The program is in need of fundamental reforms but it won't come easily.

—George Cummings, former Director, Office of Quality Control, New Hampshire Department of Health and Human Services

While New Hampshire administers the Food Stamp and TANF programs at the state-level, and my state delivers these programs at the local level, Mr. Smith's realistic view of how these programs actually work resonates across states. Similarities in the motivation and experience of commissioners or directors at the highest state (and local) levels are strik-ing.

—Joyce Johnson, former Program Manager, Employment Services, Mendo-cino County Department of Social Services, California

A well researched and written treatise that provides an insider's view of our complex welfare system. It points out the irony that a system designed to help those most vulnerable, has built-in road blocks to ensure failure. A spot on indictment of those who perpetrate the charade.

—Michael R O'Neal, former Program Manager, Stanislaus County, California

Gaudy Baubles
and Fartworms

An Insider's Guide to Welfare

TERRY R. SMITH

KHARIS
PUBLISHING

CONTENTS

PREFACE

I am not what I do. I do what I am.

You could fill a library with books written about welfare. Many of these are bulldozer books, pushing around piles of statistics. Other books are the toddler type giving mini-tantrums about how much money is spent on lazy welfare people. While some books are indignant that not enough money is being spent to support the poor, other books give nice scholarly histories of welfare. And some insinuate welfare is full of flagrant fraud.

So just what is *really* going on in welfare today? What is "welfare" anyway, and how exactly does it work...not theoretically, mind you, but how does it work in real life practical terms?

This book is a look at what's good and what's dysfunctional in our American welfare system, from the excesses of state and federal government to the games played by fartworm politicians and human services agency heads. Are you being kept distracted by gaudy baubles of pretend solutions? You deserve to be told how your money is being spent, whether it actually helps support the poor like it's supposed to, or whether it's being thrown down a rat hole with no progress to show for it.

Buckle up. This is going to piss you off.

This is everything you wanted to know about welfare but were never told. This book is about welfare like the warty toad it is, peeing in our hands.

CHAPTER 1

Some History of the Welfare Debate

I magine, if you can, a world without government welfare bureaucrats. America during the colonial period provided welfare through the philanthropic efforts of churches, charities, and towns. Everyone who helped the disadvantaged was a volunteer of sorts. Their motive was pure of heart, driven at the time by colonial Christian teaching. Volunteers who helped the poor gave their help without requiring the reams of government application forms required to apply for assistance today. In the smaller communities of that period, people were helping their neighbors.

But before we begin thinking this was a Golden Age for welfare, remember that in Colonial America the poor were put onto work farms where they labored in the fields planting crops. Nothing in principal was wrong with that, since it was to help feed themselves. But back then, widows and their children were also sold at market to the highest bidder who promised to board and room them in exchange for work. Once isolated with a farmer on his lonely property, I suspect we can guess what else some of those widows endured to protect their children. And of course, everyone back then knew that if a person was poor, they had lost God's favor, so a condition of receiving welfare often consisted of mandatory religious activities.

What changed?

In a nutshell, the Great Depression. The economic devastation that began in 1929 is still the benchmark for suffering in an America rocked back on her hob-nailed heels by something other than war. Millions of hard -working Americans became abruptly unemployed. People lost their homes, lived in travel camps, slept without supper under bridges, rode the rails looking for work, and lined up for soup in the streets. When America entered World War II a bit more than a decade later, men trying to enlist in the army were turned away because malnutrition had damaged their health.[1] Charities tried valiantly to help, but the Depression made it clear that their efforts were pitifully feeble against the volume of help needed.[2] It wasn't until after months of fumbling by Herbert Hoover, that in 1935 a new President, Franklin Roosevelt[1], pushed the Social Security Act through Congress, saving countless lives.

The Social Security Act is among our nation's most historic pieces of legislation. It introduced the grandfather of the food stamp program, which at the time simply distributed surplus agriculture goods to low income people. The Social Security Act also marked the beginning of cash assistance to support children, a program that eventually became today's Temporary Assistance to Needy Families program[2]. But the biggest change in the Social Security Act was not the programs it spawned, but that for the first time the federal government got involved in welfare programs at all. The implications of this remain hotly debated to this day.

But first, let's go even further back: to 1804, to be exact. That was the year that Lewis and Clark began their expedition to explore Thomas Jefferson's juicy real estate deal from the year before. The Louisiana Purchase included land from fifteen current states and two Canadian provinces. The acquisition of all that land resulted in the United States expanding to about 2/3rds of its current landmass. Yet the American population was only 1.7% of what it is today.

So what?

As it happens the economy of the time was primarily agriculture—small family farms. In 1804, with the Louisiana Purchase under its belt, suddenly America was swimming in land, enough land that every American for generations could go to the western frontier, clear land of trees and stones, plough, plant and harvest, and thus by the sweat of their brow become successful. From Jefferson's point of view this must have seemed an economic utopia. America was a land of seemingly unprecedented opportunity, a concept that became rooted in the American mythos.[3] But it is the nature of myths that while they can be rooted in history, they are called "myths" because they are no longer literally true.

America was rural, so welfare in America was local. Neighbors acting as agents of their church or their town, or on behalf of a charity, provided aid to members of their community who became afflicted by age, injury, disabil-

---

[1] I'm not sure Roosevelt is being given proper credit for protecting the strength of America's youth then, who would later need every shred of it to battle our enemies across both our oceans.

[2] See Appendix I "The History of the Food Stamp Program" for a longer discussion on the history of welfare.

ity, widowhood, sickness, or hunger. Bad things happen to good people. Infirmities were commonplace and their treatment uncertain at best. It was, after all, a time when the first President of the United States died, at least in part, from a cure that involved allegedly removing about half his blood over a few hours. The opinion of Americans and national leaders too—from Thomas Jefferson through Franklin Pierce and on to Herbert Hoover—was that providing welfare rightfully belonged with local communities. The federal government had no business getting involved.

Then something happened.

While early America was agricultural and much of it would remain so, the economy moved in a different direction. America industrialized. More and more, young people left family farms and took jobs as laborers in factories, as builders, as freighters, as tellers and storekeepers. In short, life evolved into what we know today. But this new economy required a whole new and much more complicated skill set than being a farmer did. As a farmer, one was self-dependent, set one's own work tasks, determined one's own schedule. But as a factory worker, an American needed a panoply of new skills, such as the ability to get along with an employer, take criticism, be at a specific place at a specific time, deal with apartment landlords, shop for food, deal with child care, find transportation to and from work. Farm life was complicated in a logistical sense, but this industrialized America was complicated in a whole new *social* way. People's work lives became a bit like modern cars: that is, more complicated and with a whole lot more that can go wrong.

Nothing illustrated this more than the Great Depression, when willingness to work hard wasn't enough. People sought jobs to feed their families, but no jobs were to be had. America was no longer the same land of opportunity we had been led to believe. We weren't Thomas Jefferson's America anymore, and this wasn't a crop failure with something as (arguably) simple as the weather to blame.[3]

Franklin Roosevelt's Social Security Act created programs of assistance that not only brought federal bread to the American jobless worker, but also acknowledged that unemployment was now a thread in the new American economic tapestry and the federal government had to be involved.

And that's where the trouble starts.

---

[3] As an interesting aside, new farmland was remote wilderness and frontier farmers were frequently isolated, which added to the already developing myth of the American hero as a strong-willed solitary loner battling against all odds. Americans should be proud of that because it was plenty true at the time.

CHAPTER 2

A Consensus of Crows

So what is "welfare" anyway? Strictly speaking, the term "welfare" began as a general term for the health and well-being of someone. The word stems from common phrases like "How fare thee?", "Fare thee well.", and "Farewell." These days, though, it has become associated with programs that provide money or other essentials like food to persons in need. Strictly speaking, "welfare" includes food stamps, cash assistance, unemployment, housing assistance, child care, Medicaid, and more.

Okay. You may have already known that. But were you aware of the variety of State programs that provide *cash* "welfare"? For our purposes here I'm not going to include federal cash programs like Supplemental Security Income (SSI) for disabled individuals, or Social Security Disability Insurance (SSDI). Both of which are administered as disability cash assistance through the U.S. Social Security Administration. Just in terms of State run programs, individuals receive State cash assistance through four primary programs:[4]

- Old Age Assistance (OAA) is a State-funded, federally mandated program for low income seniors over age sixty-five. To be eligible, a household of two OAA recipients may have no more than $712 in income per month. The OAA grant—and ANB and APTD below—are reduced by any other income to the house-hold, such as Social Security. [5]

---

[4] Data describing these programs are from 2012. I chose this time frame because that's the date when all the controversy began about restricting where and on what clients could use cash benefits. It's also before the TANF grant was adjusted in 2017. More on both of these later.

[5] Data describing these programs are from 2012. I chose this time frame because that's the date when all the controversy began about restricting where and on what clients could use cash benefits. It's also before the TANF grant was adjusted in 2017. More on both of these later.

- Aid to the Needy Blind (ANB) is a State-funded program for low income blind individuals. Income and grant data are the same as for OAA. The average grant for ANB is $183.01.
- Aid to the Permanently and Totally Disabled (APTD) is a State-funded program for low income individuals with a disability expected to last four years or longer. Income and grant data are the same as for OAA. The average grant for APTD is $152.68.
- Temporary Assistance to Needy Families (TANF) is a program for low income children. In New Hampshire, it is funded by about $38 million in federal money. To be eligible, the state must contribute about $32 million in state funds.

The Social Security Act mandates States run the OAA, ANB and APTD programs. No federal law requires states to run the TANF program, but all States do.[6]

How big are these programs? (I'm including food stamps here, despite it not being a cash assistance program *per se*.) How do they stack up relative to each other in terms of how many people are on assistance?

---

[6] Because OAA, ANB and APTD are federally mandated but state-funded, New Hampshire facilitates moving individuals to federal disability cash programs when they apply for Old Age Assistance, Aid to the Needy Blind, Aid to the Permanently and Totally Disabled, or claim a disability exemption from the work requirements for Temporary Assistance to Needy Families. Therefore, using OAA as an example, while the maximum grant is $712, federal benefits reduce the State grant such that the average OAA cash grant is $161.15.

Number of people on assistance in New Hampshire,
November 2017:

Food Stamps

Adults	53,174
Children	35,856

TANF cash

Adults	1,554
Children	5,022

Aid to the Permanently and Totally Disabled cash

Adults	6,344
Children	0

Old Age Assistance cash

Adults	1,531
Children	0

Aid to the Needy Blind cash

Adults	121
Children	1

Henceforth we're going to narrow our focus to just two of these: TANF and Food Stamps.

How do people get TANF? To be eligible for cash welfare, the TANF applicant must have a child in the household and that child must be "deprived." That is, one of the child's parents must be either absent or disabled. Some states allow the unemployment of the principal wage-earning parent as a deprivation. New Hampshire allowed that option until about 2010, when it was removed by the legislature as a cost saver.

I've often encountered confusion about who the TANF Program helps. Let's be clear about that.

To begin, we should note that 76% of TANF recipients are children. Nobody can receive TANF cash if there is not a child in the house. Note also that of the adults on assistance, 94% of them are women[7]. These are almost always mothers, with a sprinkling of grandmothers. To understand welfare, it is crucial that we take a step back to see the larger truth: When a family with children breaks up, it is almost always the mother who remains responsible for supporting the children. If the mother and her children are income eligible for welfare, it is because dad is gone and not paying child support. Maybe he's not paying because he's temporarily unemployed, maybe he's just resentful over the break up, or maybe he's just a greedy duckweed and keeps his money for himself. Or perhaps, sadly, he has passed away. Bottom line is, when we think of welfare, the first thing we should be bringing to mind is that these are women with children who should be getting help from their respective fathers, but aren't. TANF mothers have been left with all of the responsibility and no support or income.

One client explained it this way to me.

I had it all. A perfect life. My husband had a good job. We had a house and I stayed home with our three children. Then one day he just left. He emptied our bank accounts and left me with a mortgage I couldn't afford. I found myself left with three days before eviction and nowhere to live, so I wound up moving in with my new boyfriend way before we were ready.

In today's world, the term "welfare" is taking on a deeper, more sinister meaning. It is now commonly used with a tone of resentment and blame as if people using welfare are cheating the rest of us out of our hard earned paycheck. But then historically, there has been some truth to that.

That last sentence is going to stir up some of my advocate friends!

Consider this context: When Roosevelt created the cash welfare program for children in 1935, who was it serving? ... Widows, most often. Worker deaths were not uncommon as industrialization grew in America, largely unchecked by government regulations around safety protocols in logging, fishing, mining, factories, construction sites, and so on. Remember, OSHA (Occupational Safety and Health Administration) did not start until 1971. In the 1930's, America was spiritual about helping widows and orphans.

But time passed. More and more women on welfare were "never married" mothers. Increasingly children on welfare had been born out of wedlock. In

---

[7] This statistic is for New Hampshire, but rings accurately for every State.

1984, unmarried mothers represented 39% of welfare case heads. Ten years later, it was 49%. By 1998, over 57% of welfare mothers were unmarried. For Americans, this was a different moral commitment. The public became resentful as welfare gained perception as a bailout for people who made bad moral choices, rather than as a safety net for people to whom misfortune happened.

That changed everything.

Mainstream America had another point of dissatisfaction about welfare. Through the first half of the 1900's, the general consensus was that mothers should stay home to raise their children—even welfare mothers who made bad moral choices. But sentiment was building against this model, as more mothers from intact families were entering the workforce, just to help their families make ends meet. Law reflected the new reality. The Family Medical Leave Act was enacted on February 5, 1993, allowing up to a total of twelve weeks of unpaid leave following a birth during any twelve month period. How many mothers entered the workforce? In 1975, 34.3% of mothers with pre-school children under age three worked. By 2000, 61% had jobs. So the question now was, *Is it legitimate to ask working mothers to return to work after twelve weeks, only to pay taxes to allow a welfare mother to stay home with her baby?*

For most Americans, there was only one answer to that question.

By this point, the public was beginning to perceive that welfare was spiraling out of control, with "welfare queens" lazing about at home, having more babies out-of-wedlock to increase their welfare payments. Unfortunately, there was at least some truth behind this perception since states imposed zero work accountabilities on clients. But by 1964, the balance in attitude shifted into an expectation that welfare recipients should do more than just be on assistance. They should *work* to better their situation. But progress was slow. Beginning with Lyndon Johnson, each successive American President offered up some kind of work plan to "change welfare as we know it." Some tried employment programs that few states adopted. Others tried mandates on recipients that they couldn't get legislated in Congress. Others offered programs that cost too much.

By 1996 American taxpayers had had enough. Public sentiment was insistent.

Welfare mothers should work.

The public got what it wanted. In 1996, President Clinton and House Speaker Gingrich created decisive legislation that is still referred to as "Welfare Reform."[8]Among other things, it changed the name from Aid to Families with Dependent Children (AFDC) to Temporary Assistance for

---

[8] The actual bill's title was the Personal Responsibility and Work Opportunity Act of 1996

Needy Families (TANF). The term "temporary" was added to reflect the biggest change: that is, the mandate was now that able-bodied welfare adults must engage in work activities. If the activity was not actual paid employment, then it must be at least training that *led* to paid employment. States were given control of how to build TANF work programs. To fund the effort Congress block-granted federal money to States on the condition that States spend their own funds equal to what they had spent on welfare in 1995. This State share is not a match, as it is, in, say, food stamps. It's called Maintenance of Effort. In New Hampshire, the block grant was about $38 million. Our Maintenance of Effort was about $32 million.

Welfare Reform put performance measures on states. Most important among these, was the "work participation rate." Under this measure, 50% of all welfare recipients in a state—including those too disabled to work—had to be in twenty hours of work activities if the family had a child under age six, or thirty hours for those with older children. States that ran welfare programs which failed to meet a 50% work participation rate would be required to pay cash penalties back to the federal government using state dollars.

This must have solved the problem, right?

Right?

Nay. Nay, little grasshoppers. America is just not that easy. Peeling back welfare rules is a bit like peeling the rind off a stubborn orange that keeps spitting citric acid in your eye. Or peeing on an electric fence. And there are yet the gaudy baubles and fartworms to contend with. And that's where this whole thing starts getting really interesting.

The welfare reform bill had two issues. The first was that it was received with mixed results. Most Americans generally wanted wholesale change. Yet on the other hand many state bureaucrats couldn't bring themselves to impose tough accountability on welfare mothers. What, for example, to do with a mother who refused her work assignment? Do you toss them off cash assistance, an act called "full family sanction"? If you do, then doesn't the child suffer hardship? Many states in 1996—including New Hampshire—could not bring themselves to take this step, at least not before the client refused to participate for an extended period of months.

The second issue with welfare reform was that it had policy flaws. One such flaw was called the Caseload Reduction Credit. In essence, this meant that if the number of welfare recipients dropped below 1995 levels, that State would be allowed a reduction against their 50% work participation target. That is, as long as the case reductions were not caused by new restrictions on eligibility that kept people off assistance.

That sounds reasonable, right? Your state's work program is successful at getting people employed, so it should be rewarded by an easing of the 50% mandate?

Well, that's how Congress intended it, but it did not happen exactly that way. As it turned out, no one realized that at the precise moment they wrote the Welfare Reform law, America was coming out of a deep recession, meaning 1995 welfare caseloads were at historic highs. It didn't occur to Congress that as the economy improved, it was only inevitable that welfare caseloads go down. Or perhaps Clinton did realize it, and that's why he signed it—the man was, after all, brilliant. Inarguably flawed. But brilliant.

Whatever the case, the economy did begin improving almost immediately. Welfare recipients got jobs, which drove TANF caseloads down, and almost all states qualified for this "caseload reduction credit." In New Hampshire, our caseload reduction credit was forty-two points, which put our adjusted work participation target not at 50%, but 8%. And this caseload drop happened nearly everywhere in America, permitting States to ignore implementing strict work requirements on welfare mothers, while at the same time not having to worry about federal penalties. Few States hit the magic 50% work participation rate, yet only three States failed to meet their adjusted target—Arkansas, D.C., and Guam (not a state). Five states had work participation rates of 15% or lower (Arkansas and D.C. were *not* among these), but incurred no penalties.[9]

Welfare Reform had another flaw that was equally serious. While States were required to put welfare recipients into a work activity, they were not required to verify that the person actually participated in that activity for their required hours. States simply assigned recipients to an activity and then assumed they went. In the end, it's inconceivable how *any* state could have missed its work participation target.

Welfare Reform was failing. The accountability Congress had intended for States dissipated like hot breath outside in a freezing Nor'easter. Even after reform, the American welfare debate remained a political tree crowded with discontented crows, each individual crow cocking its head and throating a strident *caw...caw...caw*, an asynchronous cacophony of anxious crows. The American political din over welfare was clamoring for something better. The debate over welfare reform remained raucous.

For a time.

---

[9] (https://archive.acf.hhs.gov/programs/ofa/particip/2006/tab1a.htm)

CHAPTER 3

Work Takes...Well...Work

Welfare Reform needed a fix. Ten years after welfare reform first passed, renewal legislation still hadn't happened. Congress had extended the law some thirteen times, kicking the can down the road as the welfare debate continued to churn in Washington. On the Hill, welfare policy changes were proposed, bounced around, debated, deflated, found publicity, found obscurity. Nothing seemed to stick.

Then abruptly it did. Effective in 2006, Congress closed loopholes by enacting new welfare legislation, commonly known as TANF Reauthorization.[10] Policy was changed.

To stop states from gaming the system, the pesky caseload reduction credit was recalibrated, as to no longer be based on 1995 TANF caseloads—when numbers were high during a recession—but rather on 2005 caseloads that were much smaller. Congress allowed the caseload reduction to remain, but now it would work the way it was supposed to: that is, states could only get a credit for actually helping welfare recipients become employed. At least, that's what they thought.

Second, states were also now required to *verify* with onsite supervisors that recipients were actually participating in their work activities for their required hours. States could no longer merely assign them to activities and then look the other way.

Ultimately, it looked like this. In 1996, Welfare Reform established that welfare parents must work. But the consensus wasn't clear. States used loopholes to avoid penalty while also not implementing the intent of the law. Ten

---

[10] The technical name of the bill was The Deficit Reduction Act of 2005

years later, in 2006, TANF Reauthorization not only reiterated expectations on welfare recipients, it tightened accountabilities on states.

Seems like a clear consensus that welfare adults should work. Yes?

Nope.

Welcome to behind the scenes of welfare in New Hampshire. The way TANF Reauthorization went down here demonstrates how welfare really works.

Well, when it actually does work....

As already mentioned, New Hampshire had not implemented welfare reform in 1996. We didn't have to worry about meeting the 50% work participation requirement because we had a caseload reduction credit for the percentage decline of the caseload from pre-welfare reform. This "caseload reduction credit" was 42%. To avoid penalty, we had only to meet a net 8% participation rate. Because we never implemented the federal welfare reform law in 1996, even something as basic as our program's work activities did not match the federal list of work requirements.

In 2006, I was in charge of retooling New Hampshire's TANF program to meet the new TANF Reauthorization requirements. The first thing we had to do was build state welfare law that joined our work program activities with what federal legislation established in 1996. See below.

Federally Required Work Activities

Core Activities (20 plus hours/week)

- unsubsidized employment
- subsidized private sector employment
- subsidized public sector employment
- work experience, if sufficient private sector employment is not available
- on-the-job training
- job search/job readiness (six weeks in a fiscal year; only four weeks can be consecutive)
- community service
- vocational educational training (not to exceed twelve months with respect to any individual. No more than 30% of caseload may be deemed in this countable activity
- provision of child care to TANF recipients in a community service program

Secondary Activities (10 or less hours/ week)

- job skills training directly related to employment
- education directly related to employment, in the case of a recipient who has not received a high school diploma or certificate of high school equivalency
- satisfactory attendance at a secondary school or in a course of study leading to a certificate of general equivalence (GED), in the case of a recipient who has not completed secondary school or received such a certificate.

Any recipient under 20 counts as engaged in work if she/he maintains satisfactory attendance at a secondary school or the equivalent. No more than 30% of caseload may be deemed in this countable activity.

The Activities New Hampshire Used:
All Activities (30 hours/week)

- Work experience
- Unsubsidized employment
- Community service
- On-the-job training
- Job search/job readiness
- Post-secondary education
- Job skills training
- Adult basic education
- GED/ESL
- Barrier resolution

What follows is a sort of how-to guide for building a proper welfare work program. But it's also an example of the illogical lengths fartworms will go to block common sense government.

Buckle up.

In 2006, I was new as a Director and my New Hampshire team had to finally adapt TANF to the Welfare Reform law of 1996. We were given just eight months to make changes, a deadline of October 1, 2006. What was our starting point? Well, in terms of the work participation rate, New Hampshire's stood at between 24% and 32%...**unverified**. This meant that to meet 50% **verified** work participation, we needed to add between 600 and 700 new participants into federally countable activities. The first question, then, was

Where the heck were all our able-bodied clients? Wherever our clients were, we desperately needed to reel them back into participation with work requirements.

As we looked to modernize the program, it was imperative to take things one step at a time. First, for instance, who should be exempt from work? This is actually a tricky question. After all according to federal law, people with disabilities are included in the 50% work participation calculation, even though they are likely unable to work.

Here was a start: the exemption for having young children. In 1996, federal Welfare Reform law allowed mothers not to work for twelve months if she had a child younger than twelve months. Federal law limited that exemption to twelve months within a lifetime to ensure mothers didn't keep having babies to keep from working. But as was typical, New Hampshire chose not to adopt the federal law back then. Instead, our state went with something much more permissive, allowing mothers to be exempt from work for not twelve months, but twenty-four months. Thus, as we looked at policies implementing TANF Reauthorization in 2006, we found that about 350 moms were exempt because of children older than the federally allowed twelve months: that is, who were between the ages of twelve months and twenty-four months.

The debate?

New Hampshire's thinking back in 1996 was still apparently that mothers should remain at home with young children. But even in 1996 this thinking was already long outdated, because since 1971, *working* mothers in New Hampshire had been abiding by limits in the Family Medical Leave Act: that is, they were allowed a total of just three months of unpaid leave after giving birth. The twenty-four months allowed for welfare mothers to be paid after giving birth in New Hampshire was eight times longer than for mothers in the actual workforce. My team changed this exemption so it matched federal law. We made mothers exempt for having a child younger than twelve months. This meant welfare mothers *still* could stay home four times longer than working mothers in the general public. Granted, this revised policy was still unfair for working mothers, whose taxes pay for welfare mothers to stay home. But that's federal welfare policy, not state, and a political battle for another time

Permissive. Yes, New Hampshire's previous policy was permissive. It allowed welfare mothers to stay home with their children when mainstream mothers in the workforce couldn't. That's a fair criticism. I get that. But how exactly did that happen? How exactly did it happen that during the bulk of the 20th century, families supported themselves on one income, bought houses, prospered. The middle class thrived. Then by the 1970's, mothers and fathers felt they both had to work to get a little ahead. And so mothers increasingly did go to work. In the process, they began sending their children to day care centers and schools, as if B.F. Skinner's utopian dream was becoming reality as the community did indeed become increasingly responsible for child rearing.

These are not necessarily bad things. Mothers working may very well be more self-actualizing than a straight diet of domestic life. That should be her choice. Schools and licensed child care centers are clearly safe places for children to be, when perhaps home is in certain cases lacking learning or being abusive.

I don't want to bog us down here in an economics discussion. The point is that in today's world feeding the voracious beast to both raise children and to stay in the middle class now requires two incomes. Inflation has devoured any discretionary income that a second job used to bring families, to the point where mom staying home is not even an option in today's world, not for a family striving to stay in the middle class. Nevertheless, paying child care can eat up most of a second income, while the costs of housing, college tuition for the kids, and health care keep rising disproportionately to incomes.

The bottom line for our purposes here is, *what happens when the family is led by a single parent?* Staying at home with children is not an option for anyone anymore, least of all a TANF mom as we shall see later. Mom will have to work.

Meanwhile, New Hampshire's welfare system needed an abundance of additional fixes in order to adapt to 2006 law. Other permissive work exemptions in New Hampshire included one that exempted about sixty-six TANF mothers due to being pregnant over four months. I was not around for the policy debates in 1996, but this is another decision from the past that leaves me scratching my head. Pregnant mothers in the mainstream workforce typically work up until either delivery or health precautions stop them. In 2006, several women on my staff argued that pregnancy is not a sickness, it's a state of health. So we changed this exemption too, to make pregnant women mandatory for any suitable activity. No reason a healthy pregnant woman can't be getting a head start on a career through classroom education or skills training, for example, instead of sitting home watching TV.

Other 1996 policy choices needed reinventing. For example, a 1996 policy allowed TANF parents to receive their cash benefits *before* being asked to participate in work activities. How well did this work? About as you would expect. Nearly 70% of TANF parents did not show up for their first work-related appointment. Clearly we couldn't help people we didn't see, so we changed the law in 2006 to make an initial meeting with us a condition of eligibility. This merely meant they had to come to an orientation appointment *before* they could receive a cash benefit. From day one the statistics reversed. We went from 70% *no*-show ... to 75% *do*- show. Now we were able to teach people about the program and what it could do for them before they abandoned participating in work activities.

In addition to policy head scratchers, New Hampshire's 1996 program had built logistical issues as well. For instance, TANF clients sometimes need job readiness skills such as finding child care and transportation, how to deal with difficult people, and so on. New Hampshire had been contracting for a job readiness program that required groups of clients to enter job readiness at the same time. The "cohort" idea assumed clients would become friends, develop trust, provide each other support, and so on. Sounds good. And it was. But was it practical?

No.

The problem was it took up to six weeks before a group could be gathered and a client could actually begin job readiness training. That meant that six weeks was wasted instead of being used to make progress. Remember too that federal law had established that job readiness was limited to six weeks, only four of which could be consecutive. And by the way, the same six weeks was not just for job readiness, but also job search. Because of the time lag to get clients into the activity, and because of the time limit on job readiness and job search, New Hampshire was losing work participation credits for every one of these clients.

No more.

In 2006, we eliminated that contract model and made job readiness immediate with a strong individually driven curriculum so clients would progress without delay. We kept group activities, though, so clients still benefit from peer support.

Other logistical needs became apparent. For example, under the old 1996 TANF Program, about 236 clients were in the GED (now called HISET) activity for thirty hours. However, federal requirements only allow it as a secondary activity for ten hours (except teen parents). We had been contracting with the NH Department of Education to provide GEDs so I asked them to tell us how many clients actually attended their full thirty scheduled hours. The Department of Education answered, "Half of them."

In other words, clients were being placed in the GED activity were not doing the work, and yet were not being reassigned to a different work activity. Insult to injury, we discovered that we were paying for a full-time contracted GED facilitator in one part of our state who went an entire contract year without having a single GED referral from TANF. To this day I wonder just what the heck that person did with their time at taxpayer expense. In any case, change was in order.

GED remains important, since about 18% of TANF mothers have less than a GED. Not less a high school diploma, mind you, but less than a GED. We changed the program so that it still allowed GED full-time, and we'd eat the participation rate, but clients who didn't work at it were re -

directed to a different activity where they could be more successful, yet still have opportunity to do GED ten hours a week, if they chose.

Another logistical issue was revealed and it had to do with Job Search. Under the 1996 TANF Program, about 400 TANF adults were in job search for over four consecutive weeks. Some individuals had been in job search for two years! Since federal rules allowed job search as a countable activity for only four consecutive weeks, I found this to be another head-scratcher. Clients were being put into an activity with no real accountability. This had to change. We adapted policy so that when job search was appropriate, and when the time limit had been used, job search was an expectation on top of another, countable activity. Wise people in the mainstream workforce look for jobs while they already have them and there's no reason that's not reasonable expectation for TANF recipients as well.

And there was yet another missing management control. Untended organizations will drift. Before 2006, field supervisors in charge of welfare work counselors across the states had come to spend almost all of their time at State Office in Concord. One had drifted into being a support services expert working on billing for things like uniforms and transportation reimbursements. Another had strayed into being the computer systems advisor. This needed change. In 2006, we required field supervisors to be in the field every day directly supervising their assigned offices. We gave them cell phones so their workers could reach them with questions at any time of the day, even when they were on the road between offices. Now field workers wouldn't go months waiting for a supervisor to answer a question that might immediately impact clients and the work participation rate.

And now about that work participation rate again. Between 1996 and 2006, New Hampshire's work participation rate was 24% to 32%. But actually it was in the neighborhood of 12% to 16%.

Why?

Yet another head scratcher. Before 2006, no state in America that I'm aware of made it standard practice to verify whether TANF recipients actually participated in the activities to which they had been assigned. Yet, how is it possible to measure the success of any work activity if you don't know whether client actually attend it or how often? In 2006, my team developed a foolproof 3rd party verification system to ensure that when we placed a client into a work activity, that client went. This time around, New Hampshire was adopting the spirit of welfare reform, not creating a gaudy bauble, a fake solution of polished-up, brilliantly colored paste jewelry glittery to the uniformed eye.

Instead, we adopted the spirit of the law for reasons of our own.

One particular policy change was among the most controversial. What happens if a client refuses to participate in work? What's the right thing to do? Under New Hampshire's 1996 rules, parents who did not comply with work program requirements were allowed six months of benefits under penalty status before workers could toss them off the program.

Think about that. Welfare recipients could go a half-year not doing anything while the state worker could do little more than reduce benefits and redial the phone trying to reach clients simply so they could wheedle them toward compliance.

Accountability was so weak, abuse was so rampant, that as we've already noted 70% of clients were not even showing up to their first work related appointment. Some eventually came in, but others received six months of benefits sight unseen. Some clients were even more blatant, one telling one of my workers, "I'm going to take the summer off to be with my kids. Go ahead and sanction me." Sure enough, she did take the summer off and other than reduce her benefits there was nothing we could do about it. The 1996 reasoning behind this permissive policy was that if the case closed, the child would be without the cash safety net and that was not to be borne.

Meanwhile, let's not jump to the immediate takeaway here that TANF clients as a rule are lazy and cheat the system. On the contrary, I've met thousands of clients in my quarter-century experience. By far the majority are eager to leave TANF for a better life for themselves and their children. But then on the other hand there are always those who don't make the best choices. How's that different from the rest of Americans? Helping clients learn is one of the reasons the TANF program is here.

Still, 1996 sanctioning rules were not bringing accountability to naughtier clients, so in 2006 we responded by toughening policy. Under our new rules, clients could no longer stay on assistance for six months while refusing to participate. Instead we gave them eight weeks. If they didn't come into compliance, we closed the whole case. Full family sanction.

There had also been the problem of the revolving door. Clients sometimes closed in sanction, then reapplied for benefits promising to behave. Some got their benefits then failed to participate again, then went into sanction again, then closed again, then re-applied again. There was no management control. To solve this, we instituted a new policy in 2006. Any client who had closed for failure to participate could reapply for 100% benefits at any time, but before they could receive any benefits they first had to participate in good standing for two weeks. Skin in the game.

With all these changes in 2006, along with others, our expectations were firm. Now clients knew we were resolved about helping them and that they had to respond by helping themselves. The word on tougher sanction penalties got out and clients began immediately engaging. The number of clients in sanction did not blip up. Clients had no real problem meeting up to firm expectations.

How did all these changes work? We implemented our new TANF Reauthorization program in October 2006. The month before implementation our work participation rate was roughly 18%. The first month of implementation saw the participation rate shoot up to 24.8% *verified*. In six months, by April of 2007, our rate had reached 45.9% verified. Now, for the first time since welfare reform, clients were systemically engaging. And as a result we could actually help them.

But there was one more consequence of our new expectations we had not anticipated. In that first month of implementing the new system of accountability, the TANF caseload dropped by hundreds of cases. Turns out some clients had actually been working under the table, such as providing child care, while collecting benefits. They could do that because nobody was watching them. Now, though, they had to verify for every hour of their work requirement, so they couldn't hide what they were doing. These clients left the system. One client put it this way: "Why should I do all this free work for you. I'll just go get a real job."

Yes. Feel free to do that.

CHAPTER 4

The First Fartworm

A ll the changes we made to TANF in 2006 made sense. They were logical, they were needed, they were federal law. So when we proposed the changes, the public responded with a parade full of antique cars, fire engines, and people throwing candy to the kids lining the streets. These program changes happened to the enthusiastic applause of adoring throngs and I was written up in fanzines. After all, it was federal law, right? That meant consensus, right? Weren't New Hampshire residents excited about positive changes to their welfare system?

In point of fact, the politics involved in bringing work accountability to welfare recipients was, shall we say, "spirited."

TANF Reauthorization passed Congress and was made into law when President Bush signed it on February 8, 2006. Was it controversial? Well, all the Democrats and five republicans in the Senate voted against it. It took a tie-breaking vote by Vice -President Cheney to secure passage. That should have been a harbinger of things to come.

States were given until October 1, 2006—just eight months—to adapt their programs. What ensued was a race to change law, re-write rules, re-think policies, alter computer systems, train staff…and before any of that, develop the plan for what the new program should look like. Was New Hampshire's plan as we just described it in Chapter 3 controversial?

It was beyond controversial.

In February of 2006, who were the players in this debate? On the one hand, we had the DHHS Commissioner, my direct boss. He was a Republican and an able leader. He believed in work requirements and the intent of TANF Reauthorization. He also had the support of a comfortable Republican majority in both the New Hampshire House and Senate. Republicans rallied behind him to support TANF Reauthorization changes.

20

Ah. But the opposition. The opposition, on the other hand, was the Governor of New Hampshire, himself a Democrat. On welfare matters he turned to a trusted advisor with ostensibly impeccable credentials, none other than the previous Director of the Division of Family Assistance. My predecessor. The one who taught me about TANF in the first place.

That would also be the Director who in 1996 had framed the original TANF work programs that we were working so hard to reinvent in 2006.

Her reaction to my changes was about what you'd expect. One, she didn't want to see her program touched. Understandable, after all, since she had built it. It was her legacy. And two, it was personal because, while she was still Director of the division that I inherited from her, she left on bad terms. In a fit of pique with this new Republican Commissioner, she threatened to quit over some disagreement. Uh oh. He accepted. That's how he wound up asking me to take the job.

What follows are the behind the scenes maneuvers the public rarely gets to see. In fact, this is the first time this experience is being shared so let's get cracking, shall we? I mean, it's a hoot … especially if you're a policy wonk.

As my team created the plan for the new 2006 TANF Reauthorization program, we spent weekends writing law. I mean, at one point we literally got on our hands and knees on the marble floor just outside the Senate chamber to re-write a section of law in a compromise the Democrats had worked out with the Republican Senate President. (I've always been particularly proud of how New Hampshire's legislature manages its business so respectfully of each other's differences—well, with the exception of one House Speaker we'll refer to in the EBT chapter).

At one point during the legislative process the Governor even made a visit to my TANF staff in Manchester to ask them about our TANF Reauthorization plan. Staff gave him an earful about client abuses in a permissive system that needed changing. I think he left confused. I think he had been advised that staff felt just the opposite. Or then again maybe he was just being typically thorough. In any case, when the Republican legislature passed State law in spring of 2006 to make way for stronger work requirements in TANF, the Governor responded by letting the law pass without his signature. We implemented TANF Reauthorization in time for October 1, 2006.

Next it gets just silly.

In November, a month after implementation, New Hampshire Democrats roundly defeated Republicans in one of those infamous sweeps that reversed control of both legislative chambers—the Senate and the House. (It would happen again to Democrats themselves just two years later.) In 2006, the welfare debate had seemingly tipped on its head again.

Meanwhile, the Governor issued Executive Order 2006-8: that stated:

"A Governor's TANF Advisory Council shall be established to monitor the implementation of House Bill 1331, the Deficit Reduction Act of 2005 and this Executive Order, to advise the Governor on the need for additional changes to the TANF program, and to evaluate information provided by the Department."

In short, while Republicans pushed through a welfare law while they were in the majority, the Democratic opposition took the majority and moved to ensure those TANF changes would be minimized. The close vote in the U.S. Senate leading to the Deficit Reduction Act (TANF Reauthorization) was being played out here at home in New Hampshire.

What followed was the Governor's TANF Advisory Council giving me exhaustive, seemingly never-ending requests for data and reports. Who was Co-Chair of that Advisory Council? The previous director, the one advising both Democrats in the legislature and the Governor.

Let's be clear here. This is all exceedingly healthy. Painful for me? Yes. But also healthy. It is the democratic process in which public policy is established by majority rule, not by tyranny. Celebrate this, for it is America at its best.

Did I say it was painful?

In December of 2007, the Governor's TANF Advisory Council completed their final report and submitted it to the Governor. It was, as expected, highly critical of the changes made to TANF work programs. It was also highly inaccurate. Simply put, the primary theme of the report was to tout the relative merits of the 1996 TANF program that the previous director had built.

Well of course. Because my predecessor is the one who wrote the report.

You can't make this stuff up.

At any rate, observations and recommendations throughout the report were purposed to reverse changes to the TANF Program my team made in response to new federal law. So let's get into that a bit.

One issue that arose in the Governor's TANF Advisory Council report had to do with simple concepts of management. Since I had been made Director of the Division of Family Assistance, I had worked to orient my division more toward the science of management with clearly defined core missions, goals, objectives, and action steps. One of my earliest assessments was that clear TANF outcome targets had never been defined and therefore program success was amorphous and impossible to measure. In any vaguely constructed business environment such as this, everything becomes important, and everything is equally important. Reports erupt spontaneously to serve a momentary need, and live on uselessly measuring nothing of consequence into perpetuity to insidiously drain energy from the administration of the organization. The result is organizational drift. And it is, of course, seductively convenient that because of an absence of management controls, no data exists to deter resounding claims of success. Then claims of success will seem authentic to the uninitiated. The report prepared by the Governor's TANF Advisory Council did just that. It boasted of resounding program success under the old 1996 program.

What follows is not what you'll hear on the six o'clock news. It is a knowledgeable and thorough analysis of the kind of thinking that comprises the actual welfare debate in America. It is the in-depth policy claims by one side vs. the rebuttal and claims from the other side. But it's not just the policy back-and-forth that's important here. Equally important is how this section illustrates just how susceptible America is to obfuscation and false claims that lead to gaudy bauble solutions. I mean, who among us can really tell the difference between a scintillating piece of paste, and a real diamond? For most of us, not without a scorecard.

Strap in if you dare. Here's your scorecard.

In the second paragraph of page iii of the report, the author of the Governor's report claimed, *"From 1997 – 2004, over 20,000 New Hampshire TANF recipients were placed in jobs through the TANF program, earning the state over $31 million dollars in federal high performance bonuses."* Actually, this was not true on several levels.

- First, TANF recipients *obtained* jobs, they were not *placed in* jobs. Employment counselors in New Hampshire simply did not make job referrals. Indeed, when they were surveyed on a one month period before Reauthorization, of thirty-eight employment counselors, just one counselor had referred just one client to one job one time.
- Second, we never once earned a bonus for getting recipients jobs. Feds gave bonuses back then for three reasons:
    - ✓ how long clients stayed in jobs after leaving TANF,
    - ✓ number of clients receiving earnings gain, and
    - ✓ number of jobs people were placed in jobs.

The Department won bonuses for the first two, which were more likely measures of the health of New Hampshire's economy, which was 8th best in the country or better in years we won. We never won a bonus for placing clients in jobs.

- Third, 20,000 jobs sounds accomplished, but at the same time we were running a 50% recidivism rate, meaning half the people who left were returning back to welfare. No study had ever been conducted as to why.
- Lastly, $25 million of the $31 million in bonuses claimed had nothing to do with TANF work programs at all. Rather, $25 million of it had to do with a bonus for reducing the illegitimate birthrate in

New Hampshire. And to raise the irony to a brow-raising level of bemusement, it bears noting that the previous director who was now claiming credit for the $25 million bonus actually never intended to apply for it at all, I assume because she didn't think we would win it. I worked for her then and even I didn't know about the opportunity until two friends—federal officials—asked me why New Hampshire was not applying for the $25 million bonus. This was at a conference in Boston. She was on vacation when I returned home with just six working days to build a team, conduct research, write a methodological argument that the reduction in illegitimate birth rates was not caused by an increase in abortions, and submit a plan. We won the award by three-tenths of a percentage point.

This is a perfect example of how programs that are already confusing, can be obfuscated by false claims that seem plausible on the surface to the uninitiated. How was the Governor—or anyone else for that matter—to know better?

Management controls were mentioned in the report again: *"The Council recommends reinstating the performance measure summaries used in the past...to ensure monitoring of program success."* This was a core irritant for me, because there had never been a definition around the term "program success." In fact, once during one of my appearances before the Governor's TANF Advisory Committee, I challenged them to help me define "success." I mean, it is easy to spot the usual blithe definition that success of a welfare program is "moving clients to self-sufficiency." That's a definition you'll hear nationwide to this day. But "self-sufficiency" is only a synonym for success— and a vague one at that—so I pressed the Governor's council for a full definition of self-sufficiency. "Is it employment at minimum wage? Is it employment at the NH Living Wage? ($40,000 for a mom and two children) Is it being off government assistance?"

The answer I received? The Advisory Committee Co-Chair said that the definition of success was "too complicated," that it had to do with longevity in the workforce and long-term earnings gain. Then she said about success: "We'll know it when we see it."

"We'll know it when we see it"?

This is really the crux of the problem in any debate around public policy. For public policy to work, honest managers must create clear goals that are within the control of the organization. For instance, the federal measures of "longevity in the workforce" and "long- term earnings gain" of TANF leavers are administratively inappropriate program measures in the first place. Why? Because it's the State's economy, not the TANF Program, that predominantly determines whether the job lasts long enough for longevity to occur. The economy has to remain good for small businesses to raise wages to compete for talent, thus creating "long-term earnings gain." Using these measures alone, the best program in the country would look like historic failure in Louisiana, where the economy is perennially poor and relatively few good paying jobs are to be had. Similarly, a failing program might be mistakenly measured as highly effective in a state with an historically good economy, like New Hampshire. Yet since 1996 the federal government gave millions in taxpayer dollars to states who ranked high in these measures. In 2006, though, with TANF Reauthorization better minds in Congress prevailed and those bonuses were eliminated. Yet these measures were the ones the Governor's Advisory Committee demanded be reinstated.

Under TANF Reauthorization 2006, my team developed clear program outcomes—ones that could be measured—and linked them to a precise model of case management. One such measure was the recidivism rate. For the first time New Hampshire began development of a research tool to find out why clients returned to TANF at a 50% clip after leaving welfare for a job. We wanted to specifically learn what in their previous episode(s) on TANF may not have worked. We brought sound management controls to program administration. Program success must never, ever, be deemed as "too complicated" to define.

The Governor's Report listed other concerns. I've copied them below in italics along with my bulleted responses back to the Governor from February of 2008. It's a bit longish. But for those of you with the fortitude, this is how government *really* works.

****

1.   Third Paragraph, page iii

Though many nationally recognized experts suggested strategies which would allow states to maintain their successful programs and retain state flexibility while still meeting federal requirements, few, if any, of these allowable flexible strategies were incorporated into the NH DHHS response to reauthorization, House Bill 1331.

- First, no empiric data exists to prove that the previous program was successful even by its own undefined criteria. What does exist is the assumption that clients attended program activities, and evidence is clear that they did not: engagement of clients was minimal at 15% then, compared to 50.2% now. *[See Chapter 5 for more on this.]* Indeed, in the previous program 70% of clients failed to show for the first interview following eligibility. Now 75% do show under the current program.

- Second, the Deficit Reduction Act was a piece of federal legislation that represents the will of the American people. The Department has a responsibility not to find ways to avoid implementing law. Our responsibility is to implement legislation according to the spirit in which legislators pass it. Alternatively, State legislators have the option to pass law acquitting the Department for implementing all or part of a law based on community consensus. This has yet to happen.
- *Third, the options in the bill were not without cost.* As a "flexible strategy," the Post Employment Program, for instance, would have cost over half a million dollars for system changes alone. The post-employment program would provide ongoing benefits to people who normally would have closed. *Assuming a $200 grant, the cost of the post-employment program option would be another $3,100,800 a year in new expenses at a time when the TANF Reserve is already being deficit spent by $10 million a year.*

2.   Paragraph 1, page iv

The average number of clients meeting the federal requirements for participation in FFY 2004 was 1,024, yielding a participation rate of 30.2%.

- Again, this pre-Reauthorization number is how many clients were simply assigned to activities, unverified. Experience and survey indicate that half of these clients actually did not attend the activities.

We are concerned that we do not know how many families dropped off the program due to an inability to meet new TANF requirements.

- It may help balance the issue to reframe this statement in other ways. For example:
  ✓ We also do not know how many families dropped off the program due to a refusal to meet new TANF requirements because they are now accountable to attend activities, not just be assigned. (Clients commonly tell us about the thirty hour work requirement, "I am not going to work for free.")
  ✓ We also do not know how many clients were beneficiaries of an informal economy: that is, how many lived with boyfriends and had no intention ever of going to work.
  ✓ We also do not know how many clients previously worked under the table, such as providing child care in their home for

unreported income, hence would have been income ineligible if they told us, so preferred to let their case close.

- The Department would be happy to conduct a Leaver study of people who have left TANF, but the last such contract with UNH cost over a $1 million and due to structural issues was never released.

Ultimately, the principal difference between the old program and the new program is that this new program is much more demanding of clients. Able-bodied recipients may no longer sit at home on TANF. They are now faced with a choice of working thirty hours through employment for pay, or working thirty hours for a TANF cash benefit. Since they can earn more through a job, it is clear that a significant caseload reduction is to be expected. Indeed, most of the caseload reduction happened within the first month of TANF Reauthorization.

3. Penalties for Not Complying with Work Requirements, page iv

From the data available, the percent of clients sanctioned has increased slightly, but cases closing due to sanctions are substantially higher, and hundreds of cases have been denied for not meeting new policy requirements.

- First, this new TANF Program is about engagement. The Department cannot assist clients we do not see.
- Federal requirements in the Deficit Reduction Act shifted the program to mandatory participation in the federally restricted array of activities. Add to this that each client's participation for every hour of every day of every week of every month must be third party verified. Clients (and workers) had to undergo a severe culture shift that moved clients from enablement, to empowerment.
- It demonstrates clear success of the program that despite the considerable new accountabilities on clients, the number of clients failing to comply is only slightly higher than when there were few demands placed on them. Yet the participation rate, that is the engaging of clients, is improved from 30% **unverified**, to 50.2% **verified** in the first year.
- Prior to Reauthorization, clients who were noncompliant and put into sanction, merely promised to comply and were allowed back into the program. This created a revolving door for individual clients coming and going who never intended or attempted to comply. At the request of Department workers, the new requirement is that every sanctioned client must comply for two weeks, at which

time the sanction is entirely lifted. Note that the individuals who close in sanction, and who are subsequently denied as stated above, a) never cured their sanction by complying for two weeks, and b) had ten weeks to do so before closing. These would be people who, in the old program, never engaged.

We have learned that many cases are closed without the home visit established to determine whether a client can't or won't cooperate with work requirements, and that visits are not taking place soon enough in the process to avoid closure.

- We appreciate the concern that visits are not taking place as soon as they might. That is why the Department improved the process and changed these visits from occurring in the 5th month, as under the old program, to the 5th week under the new. Waiting five months to learn of a problem with participation was a disservice to clients.
- The contractor providing home visits is Child and Family Services, a highly responsible agency who calls every sanctioned client in the 5th week. However, not all clients continue to reside at their old address, and many have not reported their new whereabouts. Moreover, the Department does not have—nor should have—the authority to mandate the client allow us into their home, and many if not most clients refuse this entry.

4. **Assessment of Client Circumstances, last paragraph, page iv.**

Assessment of client circumstances—such as mental or physical disabilities— must take place and be considered before clients are penalized for non-compliance or placed in an activity.

- First, we already ask questions about disabilities and family violence in the eligibility process. Barriers are explored in the work program case management process. However, if clients choose not to disclose, the Department cannot know of such circumstances.
- Second, basic life skills is also already a part of the case management continuum. Yet when clients refuse to participate in the program, they go into sanction. There is a logical disconnect here that we can somehow ensure people have basic life skills who refuse to attend activities designed to provide them.

5. **Vocational Training and Other Activities**

The Governor's TANF Executive Order requires the Department to "increase, up to the federally allowable maximum, the number of individuals taking part in vocational training and education." This was not done.

- There is no disincentive, as the report seems to imply, for the Department *not* to place individuals in training activities. Indeed, training is a countable activity for federal participation purposes. At issue here is the assumption that the Department has the authority to impose training or education on clients who do not opt for it.

- Again, the principal misunderstanding here is that the 11.3% baseline participation in training in FFY 2006 is in any way an accurate portrayal of need. ***Remember, the 11.3% participation cited for 2006 is based on unverified participation. Our experience demonstrates that prior to Reauthorization, only about half of people assigned to activities actually attended. This would mean that, because it is verified actual attendance, the 6.8% participation in training in FFY 2007 is actually comparable to, or more favorable than, the previous year's 11.3% unverified.*** We reiterate that comparisons of the two programs are not possible given the distinctly different business environments of each.

- Nevertheless, the Department is working on an innovative pilot in Laconia around training. Business Basics with Career Success Tracks is a three-tier vocational skills training program that is being piloted in Laconia in collaboration with the Laconia Community Technical College, WIA, and DFA/NHEP. Tier One consists of eleven weeks of accelerated college studies in Software Applications, Foundations of Writing, Fundamentals of Math, and Intro to Professional Business Practice. It culminates in ten college credits and a Certificate of Proficiency. Tier Two consists of Career Track On-The-Job Training placement into employment within an office environment of the student's choice of industry sector, such as health care, finance, human services. Concurrent with the OJT employment and in support of continued career and wage wage growth, Tier Three consists of Career Track Continued Education in a college course consistent with the student's career goals. As an example, for finance careers there might be an accounting course. The program is funded through a combination of TANF and WIA [Workforce Investment Act] funds.

The life skills program which taught parenting skills, money management, balancing work and family and using community resources was eliminated on September 30, 2006.

- This is not true. Actually the life skills program referred to was not eliminated, it was replaced. A new contractor providing better outcomes has been hired for the same purposes, but with three added distinctions. One, clients are not refused access for six weeks while waiting for a classroom opening. Two, classroom training is integrated with a work attachment component. Third, the TANF program no longer duplicates payment of over $100,000 with state dollars for nutrition education through the life skills contract, since it has for twenty years been part of a federal food stamp grant serving the same population.

6.   Program Costs, page v

Given the numbers of clients participating is well below the original estimate, the increased use of funding does not appear to be justified.

- Again, a fundamental misunderstanding about TANF Reauthorization here is that it may not be compared easily to the program the feds allowed before. The task of working with clients to attain verifications of every hour of participation, of every day of every week of every month, is administratively enormous, and requires specialized positions to help with this so employment counselors can do more counseling around employment.

- Still, given the restrictions on spending, the Department is reviewing contracts and other expenditures for opportunities for savings.

7. Data, page vi

The Local Welfare Administrators' Association has been unable to determine if a cost shift to towns and cities has occurred because DHHS has not provided the information on denied and closed clients that NHLWAA sought to make a determination if TANF program changes caused any additional costs to towns and cities.

- This is not a true statement. In point of fact, the Department and the Local Welfare Administrator's Association have met on this issue. The problem isn't that the Department isn't willing to work with towns, but rather that the Towns have decided they do not have baseline data on their TANF clients that can be used to measure whether there has been an increase due to Reauthorization.

(Simply providing cost per town and assuming it is all due to Reauthorization, rather than subtracting out costs which were common **before** Reauthorization, is administratively unacceptable as a program measurement tool.) The Department remains available and open to any continued discussion around this issue, historically meets with Town Welfare Association Executive Committee monthly, and continues to convene representatives of the Town Welfare Association with the Commissioner and senior management quarterly.

8. Last Paragraph, p vi.

Maintaining ongoing outcome measures and ranking New Hampshire on a national basis allows our legislature and public to see how the TANF Program is working. This information is needed to evaluate program success and it should be freely provided.

- Actually outcome measures are being conducted in a way that ranks New Hampshire on a national basis. Already, New Hampshire has been held up as a national model for implementation of TANF Reauthorization. We have been invited to speak on our success to over half the states in the U.S. Clearly the theme once again here is that the Report does not agree with the Deficit Reduction Act and chooses not to define "program success" the way the law intended it to be.

****

In the end, it played out like this. As is the case with all New Hampshire Commissioners, the Republican Commissioner I'd worked with to fix welfare in 2006 had a four year term limit. His term expired and as expected the Democratic Governor appointed someone new. The Governor's TANF Advisory Council completed their massive report in late 2007/early 2008, about eighteen months after we implemented our TANF Reauthorization changes.

Here it continues to be interesting.

When the report was first written, the Governor handed it to his new hand-picked Commissioner, my new boss, for review before making it public. Being recent to welfare generally, the new Commissioner passed it down to me for comments, the ones you've just read (or perhaps had the good sense not to).

Now, let's be clear about the dynamics at play here. This was a new Commissioner who wanted to please his new boss. He was eager to support the

Governor's report. But as you've seen above the report was riddled with factual inaccuracies and my review of it was frank. When this new Commissioner finished reading my review, he told me how disappointed he was with me and from there our relationship soured and basically never recovered.

Well, disappointment cuts both ways, I guess.

And that brings us back to where we began. Instead of volunteers from churches, charities and towns providing assistance to the poor, in today's world government hires people who make it their careers. As for me, I was career. I could have gotten in solid with the new Commissioner and cemented my career by simply going-along-to-get-along. Keep the wheels turning, no matter the direction. I mean, that's what he was doing. All I had to do was abandon the truth and my integrity.

Easy peasy.

As I've said, Democrats swept into office immediately following implementation of TANF Reauthorization. They eventually passed another TANF bill, SB 226, but it had only one change of consequence to the actual administration of the program. It increased the length of time it took to close a TANF case for noncompliance, from eight weeks to ten weeks. Hardly the six months it had been before, meaning the bi -partisan debate was largely settled in this and all regards. The opposition had reviewed my ideas and determined them to be solid.

And that is the nature of debates in America. The stars must align with infinitesimal perfection for public policy to budge. First there is the debate itself that must inspire policy makers to understand both sides of it. Then there must be policy-makers with legislative power to push it through. Then the public must have some interest to generate the political will in the first place to make policy makers pay attention. And then, even after all those things align, it only takes a fartworm bureaucrat whispering half-truths and fake news into the right ears to put the white liquid pigeon poop on any practical solution. As it was, welfare Reform in 1996 stalled in most states because one of these stages went *kablooey*.

So it goes. In the end, New Hampshire's Governor never released the report to the public and TANF was left intact with its improved program.

Where does all this leave us?

For one thing, let's not rush to judge the Governor. He was, in my estimation, a very intelligent, middle-roader trying to do the right thing and astute enough to recognize that casting a stone into the pond sends ripples to all shores. In fact, he's someone I admire, and I confess to be pretty grudging about permitting myself to imbue that label. He did what Governors are supposed to do: he delegated responsibility to people he trusted to be experts. This time I can only imagine he ultimately learned he had been led up a talus slope so he extricated himself as gracefully as he could without abandoning his base. He's not the fartworm here, if that's what you were thinking. Governors and Commissioners need people with the integrity to tell them the truth, even when they don't want to hear it, don't appreciate it, and punish it. The governor hadn't benefited from that kind of truth until he had already been led down a sewer hole and caught his first scent of septic stench when he read my review of his Advisory Council's report.

The good news?

Sometimes to stars do align. They did in New Hampshire.[11]

---

[11] Another illustration of this is how the Food Stamp Program began. If you're interested, see Appendix A for a brief "History of the Food Stamp Program."

CHAPTER 5

TANF: The Ghost in the Doorway...Haunting...Invisible...Stranded in Reality

Across the country, State welfare agencies are caught in a trap. On the one hand, they must implement federal welfare work requirements and meet federal outcomes such as 50% client work participation. On the other hand, many State welfare agencies face stiff resistance from their own legislators, service providers and advocates who are not in agreement with strict work requirements. Point being, passage of Federal law does not mean consensus. On the contrary, the welfare debate is still playing itself out in States across America, but it happens so invisibly you don't get a serious vote in the matter.

Here are a couple of things fartworms don't want you to know for the simple reason you'll be pissed off like me. And what is seriously wrong here is that State and even federal bureaucrats find ways to skirt the mandates of federal law. Take this for example.

To begin, let's recap a few things. In 1996, Congress passed law requiring States to bring a work a requirement to welfare recipients. States were to be measured according to whether 50% of all welfare recipients on cash assistance were in a specific list of work activities for a specified number of hours. Yet from 1996 to 2006 States used a gimmick called "the caseload reduction credit" to avoid implementing firm accountabilities on clients. Then in 2006 Congress passed TANF Reauthorization, reiterating and reinforcing work requirements in TANF. The 50% work participation rate became more real.

Did it work?

First, what exactly is the Work Participation Rate? The federal requirement is that 50% of all TANF adults receiving cash and under age sixty must be in one of the federal work activities listed in Chapter 3. A person is exempt

if they are caring for a child under age one, but only for twelve months lifetime. Individuals are included in the 50% calculation even when they not be
physically disabled and cannot work.

What?

Uh huh. If a client is too disabled to work, and can prove it through a
doctor's verification, they still count against the State's work participation
rate.

Even so, States can achieve this rate. But some States, even twenty years
after welfare reform first passed, haven't figured it out. Here are tables showing national work participation rates from 2013 through 2016.

National Work Participation Rankings
FFY 2013
Red is Federal Penalty

Ranking	State	Participation Rate
1	Wyoming	79%
2	Maine	77%
3	New Hampshire	76%
4	North Dakota	74%
5	Illinois	69%
6	Mississippi	63%
7	Georgia	62%
8	South Dakota	57%
9	Kentucky	55%
10	Michigan	53%
11	New Mexico	52%
12	Nebraska	51%

Ranking	State	Participation Rate
13	Idaho	51%
14	Ohio	51%
15	Maryland	50%
16	Alabama	49%
17	Connecticut	48%
18	Massachusetts	47%
19	Oregon	47%
20	Hawaii	47%
21	Minnesota	45%
22	Florida	45%
23	District of Columbia	44%
24	North Carolina	44%
25	Virginia	43%
26	Alaska	43%
27	Montana	40%
28	Arkansas	40%
29	Delaware	39%
30	Vermont	39%
31	West Virginia	37%
32	Iowa	36%
33	Nevada	36%

Ranking	State	Participation Rate
34	Guam	36%
35	Wisconsin	34%
36	Indiana	33%
37	Kansas	32%
38	New York	32%
39	South Carolina	32%
40	Utah	30%
41	Tennessee	29%
42	Oklahoma	27%
43	Pennsylvania	26%
44	California	25%
45	Colorado	24%
46	Louisiana	24%
47	Missouri	22%
48	New Jersey	22%
49	Puerto Rico	22%
50	Arizona	21%
51	Texas	20%
52	Virgin Islands	16%
53	Washington	13%
54	Rhode Island	12%

National Work Participation Ranking
FFY 2014
Red is Federal Penalty

Ranking	State	Participation Rate
1	New Hampshire	78%
2	Wyoming	72%
3	North Dakota	71%
4	Maine	69%
5	Illinois	68%
6	Mississippi	64%
7	Michigan	62%
8	Ohio	60%
9	Massachusetts	58%
10	Georgia	57%
11	South Dakota	57%
12	Kentucky	57%
13	Alabama	52%
14	Oregon	52%
15	Maryland	50%
16	Idaho	50%
17	Nebraska	48%
18	Hawaii	48%

Ranking	State	Participation Rate
19	Connecticut	47%
20	Minnesota	46%
21	District of Columbia	45%
22	Florida	45%
23	Virginia	44%
24	Montana	43%
25	West Virginia	42%
26	Arkansas	42%
27	Alaska	42%
28	Vermont	41%
29	New Mexico	39%
30	North Carolina	38%
31	Guam	37%
32	Iowa	36%
33	Wisconsin	36%
34	South Carolina	35%
35	Delaware	35%
36	Kansas	34%
37	New York	32%
38	Nevada	31%
39	Indiana	30%

Ranking	State	Participation Rate
40	California	30%
41	Tennessee	27%
42	Oklahoma	25%
43	New Jersey	25%
44	Pennsylvania	24%
45	Louisiana	23%
46	Colorado	23%
47	Utah	21%
48	Puerto Rico	21%
49	Missouri	20%
50	Arizona	19%
51	Texas	18%
52	Washington	16%
53	Virgin Islands	15%
54	Rhode Island	12%

TANF Work Participation Rates: National Ranking

Ranking	State	Participation Rate
1	New Hampshire	79%
2	Wyoming	72%

Ranking	State	Participation Rate
3	Maine	71%
4	Michigan	69%
5	North Dakota	68%
6	Oregon	68%
7	Illinois	66%
8	Idaho	65%
9	Mississippi	63%
10	Georgia	62%
11	Massachusetts	60%
12	South Dakota	58%
13	Ohio	57%
14	California	56%
15	Kentucky	55%
16	Alabama	54%
17	Maryland	52%
18	District of Columbia	50%
19	Connecticut	50%
20	Florida	45%
21	Hawaii	45%
22	Virginia	45%
23	Arkansas	44%

Ranking	State	Participation Rate
24	Vermont	44%
25	Nebraska	43%
26	West Virginia	42%
27	Montana	40%
28	Alaska	40%
29	Wisconsin	39%
30	Minnesota	38%
31	Nevada	38%
32	Iowa	37%
33	South Carolina	37%
34	New Mexico	36%
35	Kansas	35%
36	Delaware	33%
37	New York	32%
38	Indiana	30%
39	Arizona	30%
40	Tennessee	27%
41	New Jersey	27%
42	Pennsylvania	25%
43	Oklahoma	24%
44	Missouri	22%

Ranking	State	Participation Rate
45	Louisiana	21%
46	Texas	20%
47	Washington	20%
48	North Carolina	20%
49	Colorado	18%
50	Puerto Rico	19%
51	Guam	16%
52	Utah	16%
53	Rhode Island	15%
54	Virgin Islands	12%

TANF Work Participation Rates: National Rankings. FFY 2016

Ranking	State	Participation Rate
1	Maine	87%
2	New Hampshire	80%
3	Oregon	73%
4	Illinois	72%
5	Wyoming	72%
6	North Dakota	68%

Ranking	State	Participation Rate
7	Michigan	65%
8	Massachusetts	64%
9	Mississippi	61%
10	California	61%
11	Idaho	60%
12	South Dakota	58%
13	Georgia	57%
14	Alabama	56%
15	New Mexico	55%
16	Ohio	52%
17	District of Columbia	50%
18	Vermont	48%
19	Connecticut	47%
20	Kentucky	46%
21	Virginia	45%
22	Arkansas	45%
23	Nebraska	45%
24	Florida	44%
25	Wisconsin	42%
26	Kansas	42%
27	South Carolina	41%

Ranking	State	Participation Rate
28	Hawaii	41%
29	Montana	40%
30	Minnesota	39%
31	Alaska	39%
32	Delaware	38%
33	West Virginia	37%
34	Iowa	37%
35	Nevada	35%
36	Tennessee	34%
37	Maryland	33%
38	New York	31%
39	Washington	32%
40	Arizona	31%
41	Indiana	30%
42	Oklahoma	31%
43	New Jersey	27%
44	Missouri	27%
45	Pennsylvania	26%
46	North Carolina	22%
47	Texas	22%
48	Colorado	20%

Ranking	State	Participation Rate
49	Guam	19%
50	Puerto Rico	18%
51	Rhode Island	15%
52	Louisiana	14%
53	Utah	12%
54	Virgin Islands	12%

The secret—and now you know it—is that a state like Utah with a 12% work participation rate (2016) *did not* earn a federal penalty and that a state with a 20% work participation rate *does* earn a federal penalty. Yet neither State meets the 50% target mandated in law. It all boils down on how good the State is at gaming the system.

But there's more.

Look at each chart above. All the states in red? All of them incurred a federal financial penalty for poor performance regarding the mandatory 50% work participation rate. The law indicates they should be punished for poor performance that for some of them is habitual and extends back for years. For instance in 2007 fifteen States failed to meet the 50% work participation rate target, even with the option to use the variety of new loopholes.

I'm going to be honest here. I guided New Hampshire into using loopholes too. One loophole, for instance, is to provide a $20 TANF benefit to food stamp families that have children and are employed at least thirty hours a week. The benefit can be used for food only, but has the advantage of allowing the State to count the family toward the work participation rate. I didn't like doing it that way. But it was legal and protected New Hampshire from penalty because...who knows...maybe the feds will call in those debts someday.

But probably not. As of this writing, the federal government has failed to hold any State going back to 1996 accountable for actually paying a financial penalty. Twenty years of poor performing states and not one has been held accountable to the law.

This is the real enemy of the American democracy. State administrators get away with scoffing at the law of the land. Regardless which side of the debate you land on here—and frankly, I agree with almost all the experts that a 50% work participation rate is not a valid measure of States' management of the TANF Program—but the law is the law. Either change it…or adopt it. Otherwise our government is, as many disillusioned individuals in the general public believe, simply a scruffy bunch of fartworm bureaucrats taking 20% of our income through taxes only to hoodwink us as to how they're spending it and what we're getting for it.

And that's just federal taxes.

I mean, really? Twenty years since Welfare Reform and States still don't get it right?

CHAPTER 6

What Are They Hiding from You in the Food Stamp Program (SNAP)?

W e're going to take a slight detour from TANF here to make a point about the dishonesty of public servants in the Food stamp Program. This is a program designed to feed hungry Americans. So how bad can it be?

One of the gaudiest baubles ever.

At this writing, utter mismanagement of the Food Stamp Program exists at the highest levels of the federal USDA Food and Nutrition Service where unscrupulous career people have been busy falsely branding the program in nothing less than a conspiracy to mislead Congress about fraud, waste and abuse. Frankly it's a scandal that should have rocked the nation instead of just barely making local news in a few affected states. It may still rock the nation.

This is going to take slogging through a bit of detail. Better belt yourself in. It's worth it.

Like TANF, the Food Stamp Program has its own outcome measures linked to federal law. One big one is called the "Error Rate." Simply put, the error rate is the ratio of total food stamps issued in a year compared to the total dollars issued by mistake, or "in error." Whether the state erroneously issues a dollar too much, or a dollar too little, either way it is a dollar issued in error. Nor does it matter whether the error is caused by a state worker's administrative mistake, or is caused by the client's failure to tell us about a new job. In the end, the State's error rate is computed by taking its total food stamp issuance compared to error issuances. Let's say a State issues $1 million in a year. Of this issuance, let's say $100,000 was either over-issued or under-issued. That state would have an error rate of 10%.

How do we know about errors? Here's how the system works.

Eligibility for food stamps begins with applicants telling the State about their financial circumstances. To ensure truth telling, the State verifies client finances with "third parties." This means income and expense forms are sent to employers, landlords and so on to be directly filled out by them. State workers can accept employer check stubs for earnings in the most recent pay periods too. To make sure the client is disclosing everything, State workers also double-check against electronic crossmatches with other state and federal agencies, such as New Hampshire Employment Security's New Hire report, wage report, and unemployment insurance report. Other automatic crossmatch reports include matching with the Social Security Administration for Social Security Number (identity), Social Security Income, and Social Security Death Match. The Internal Revenue Service is a mandatory match partner also (even though the information is so old as to be useless). And…sometimes…in addition to third-party verifications and crossmatches…sometimes our eligibility workers just simply have an uneasy sense of fraud. They have a gut feeling that something is not right about the case. When that happens they refer the case to the Office of Special Investigations who does a deeper review. This process is systematized into the application process as "FRED," or Front End [Fraud] Detection. Also a Fraud Hotline is published on the Department's website for community members to call if they wish to report fraud that has come to their attention. Lastly, eligibility is not determined just once. Rather, in most cases eligibility is completely re-determined every six months, including another client interview and mandatory updated verifications of all financial information.

There's more.

Eligibility does not end with the opening of a case. Rather, eligibility determinations and re-determinations are subject to a three-tier case review process. First, once eligibility has been determined, the eligibility worker's supervisor does a worker sampling for case reviews to ensure accuracy and enters results in a case review data base used to track worker performance and areas of weakness. The more novice the worker, the more frequent the case reviews. Second, after eligibility our Quality Control Unit (QC) selects a random, statistically valid sampling of cases for a complete review, which includes another interview of the client usually in the client's home, and poring over the case record of verifications and crossmatches. Third, once Quality Control is done with a case, a sub-sample of QC's sample is selected and a second round of reviews is conducted by reviewers from the USDA Food and Nutrition Service, the federal agency that oversees SNAP, who look for not only accuracy in the original case, but whether the state's QC system is operating correctly.

Upshot is, from all this we have a strong understanding of the prevalence of fraud in SNAP. In New Hampshire, the Quality Control Unit reviewed 704 cases in 2016. Of these, twenty cases were found in client error, meaning the client-caused SNAP case error rate for 2016 was 2.8%. And of this fraction, most were found not to be intentional. Thus the SNAP fraud rate is empirically deemed to be in the under 1% range.

Okay. So all that sounds pretty thorough and foolproof, right? How could it all go sideways?

Here's the problem. Simply put, the USDA gives States $ 48 million in high performance bonuses each year, per federal regulations at 7 CFR 275.24(a). But here's the kicker. States earn their federal cash bonuses by competing against each other for the lowest error rate. In short, States have financial incentive to misrepresent their error rates.

And that's exactly what happened.

In about the year 2000, a consulting business called the Rushmore Group began offering itself as a hired gun to teach States how to lower their food stamp error rates. Later Julie Osnes, a founding member of that firm, branched out on her own. Julie Osnes Consulting insists the firm merely showed States how to interpret obscure federal rules around quality control in a way that would get them out of food stamp errors. But according to the Department of Justice in a news release from April 10, 2017, she advised the use of:

> ...several improper and biased quality control practices, including: (1) finding a basis for dropping error cases from the review by discouraging beneficiaries from cooperating with information requests and pursuing unnecessary information; (2) selectively applying requirements and policies to overturn and reduce errors; (3) asking beneficiaries leading questions to obtain desired answers to eliminate error potential; (4) arbitrating any and all differences with USDA; (5) subjecting error cases to additional scrutiny and quality control casework with the goal of overturning an error or dropping a case; and (6) omitting verifying information in documents made available to USDA.

But to what effect?

Once Osnes started overhauling the integrity of State Quality Control units, she got results and the flood gates opened. Over the years about two dozen States engaged Osnes to help them hide food stamp mistakes from the feds. Results were startling. In 2000, the national food stamp error rate averaged 8.91%. By 2014 this had been reduced to 3.66%. This improvement was not based on real performance, but rather—according to the Department of Justice—a performance enhanced by a sort of illegal quality control steroid [my image, not DOJ's].

But what's most disturbing here is that the food stamp feds—the USDA Food and Nutrition Service—knew exactly what was going on, but refused to admit it or to look into it. I know this because I was raising the issue to them every chance I got beginning in 2008. So was my good friend George Cummings, who was New Hampshire's Quality Control Director at the time. New Hampshire did not play in that particular litter box.

What gave the corruption away?

Math doesn't lie. In 2006 Florida's error rate was 8.59%. The national average was 5.99%. Florida was facing a federal financial penalty and had to take some action because, unlike TANF, the food stamp feds actually made States pay up on their penalties. So Florida hired Julie Osnes and the next year their error rate halved. Then in 2008, their error rate dropped to 0.85%.

This is more than statistically improbable.

Why? Because not only did Florida's workers sprout angel wings as they became all but perfect, *but their clients never caused errors either.* It's this latter part that is particularly damning. Before Osnes Florida's 2006 client-caused error rate was 5.04%. But by 2008, the client error rate dropped to 0. 42%. The next year it was down to 0.19%. Apparently food stamp recipients in Florida didn't make mistakes, never lied, and never forgot to report a change in income beyond the ten days allowed to do so.

What was Florida's payoff? Bonus money. Lots and lots of bonus money.

Year	Bonus Dollars
2007	$5,4811,910
2008	$7,179,612
2009	$11,552,247
2010	$6,083,577
2011	$9,087,687
2012	$8,072,238
2013	$7,015,422

In all, Florida profited from the Osnes relationship by a whopping total of $42,524,271. They grew so confident, a Florida representative told me and a roomful of State and federal Food Stamp administrators at a Washington State conference that the State actually put bonus money in their budget.

Meanwhile, Osnes was getting a cut of the bonuses.

Other States benefited from the Osnes miracle: Alaska, Washington State, California, South Carolina, Colorado, Texas, Missouri, Wisconsin, Georgia, Michigan, Indiana, Tennessee, Mississippi, Louisiana, Nebraska, Alabama, Maine, Pennsylvania, Rhode Island, Connecticut, New Jersey, Delaware, District of Columbia, and Virginia. Osnes States controlled the entirety of the federal performance bonus pool. Osnes States were raking it in, a consultant (Osnes) was getting rich, and the food stamp feds were bragging to Congress about how amazing a job they were at bringing integrity to the biggest welfare program.

Integrity. That word became the pepper shaker whose cap pops off over your food.

Am I saying definitively that Florida cheated? No. Of course not. How could I, since the USDA Food and Nutrition Service paid the way for State after State to go to Florida to visit the error rate miracle there? I was sent on that tour too. While I was there, Florida made no mention in my hearing of Julie Osnes. And so far (note I make a dutiful disclaimer) the Department of Justice has not formally determined them to be in non-compliance with federal standards.

But does that mean a comeuppance is not forthcoming? Who knows. But rumors are indeed flying around that (as of this writing January 2018) Florida is not only being investigated, but that criminal charges are being considered. Of course these rumors gather strength and have some special volatility among the half of America, the non-Osnes States, whose bonus and penalty fortunes suffered bleak fortune over the Osnes years. But more on that in a moment.

Some mainstream national press have picked up the story, but only in certain affected states has it made anything akin to a stir. The Department of Justice began an investigation that, according to some reports, remains ongoing among Osnes States. Wisconsin was investigated and determined to be acting improperly. They have been ordered to pay back $7 million in high performance bonus money accrued through following advice from Osnes Consulting:

> As part of the settlement, WDHS [Wisconsin Department of Human Services] admitted that, beginning in 2008, it utilized the services of Julie Osnes Consulting, a quality control consultant, to review the error cases identified by WDHS quality control workers. WDHS further admitted that based on instructions from Julie Osnes Consulting it implemented several improper and biased quality control

practices, including: (1) finding a basis for dropping error cases from the review by discouraging beneficiaries from cooperating with information requests and pursuing unnecessary information; (2) selectively applying requirements and policies to overturn and reduce errors; (3) asking beneficiaries leading questions to obtain desired answers to eliminate error potential; (4) arbitrating any and all differences with USDA; (5) subjecting error cases to additional scrutiny and quality control casework with the goal of overturning an error or dropping a case; and (6) omitting verifying information in documents made available to USDA. These practices improperly decreased WDHS's reported error rate, and as a result, WDHS earned performance bonuses for 2009, 2010, and 2011 to which it was not entitled.

Virginia was investigated with a similar finding, and was also ordered to pay back $7 million in high performance bonus money.

As part of the settlement, VDSS [Virginia Department of Social Services] admitted that, beginning in 2010, it retained Julie Osnes Consulting, a quality control consultant, to reduce its SNAP benefits determination error rate by training VDSS quality control workers to "use whatever means necessary" to find a benefits decision "correct" rather than finding an error. VDSS also admitted that if its quality control staff "could not find a way to make a benefits decision correct," they were instructed to "find a reason to 'drop' the case, or eliminate it from the sample." VDSS acknowledged that this outcome-driven method, as implemented by VDSS between 2010 and 2015, "injected bias into the case review process" because it was designed to lower VDSS's reported error rate by falsely reporting errors as "correct" or eliminating them from the sample. Through its use of these biased methods, VDSS was improperly awarded USDA performance bonuses for 2011, 2012, and 2013.

VDSS further admitted that VDSS quality control workers did not want to use the methods proposed by Julie Osnes Consulting because they believed the methods lacked integrity, injected bias into the quality control process, and violated USDA requirements, and that they communicated these concerns to their supervisors. VDSS admitted that the former VDSS quality control manager pressured and intimidated these employees to force them to adopt these methods, including, according to these employees, threatening termination, providing negative performance reviews, taking away teleworking and flexible scheduling privileges, and engaging in other forms of harassment and retaliation. (http://dakotafreepress.com/tag/julie-osnes)

The DOJ also investigated Alaska, which was ordered to pay back $2.5 million:

> "Alaska, like many other states, relied on a contractor, (Julie) Osnes Consulting, who advocated practices that may have led to the inaccurate reporting of food stamp error rates to USDA," the department said in an email response to questions. "USDA awarded bonuses between 2010 and 2014 based on the reported error rates."
> Alaska in late 2009 hired Julie Osnes Consulting LLC, a South Dakota_firm. The consultant injected bias into the quality control process for the program, known as SNAP, the Justice Department said. (https://www.usnews.com/news/best-states/alaska/articles/2017-09-18/alaska-to-pay-25m-to-settle-false-claims-in-food-program)

We should take a brief pause here to note that a spokesman for Mike Conaway (R-Texas), who for years was Chairman of the House Agriculture Committee, said he is "monitoring the investigation".[12] It bears also noting that the Representative's own home state, Texas, became an Osnes state late in the process. In 2009, Texas sported a 6.90% error rate when the national average was 4.36%, putting them in financial penalty with the food stamp feds. The next year their error rate was 2.93% and their client error rate dropped from 2.77% to 0.76%.

Let's just stop here. Re-read that. The "client" error rate dropped from 2.93% down to 0.76%. Again, that is not just statistically improbable, it seems statistically impossible. Texas, Florida, and all other states can claim control over the performance of government workers. But food stamp recipients? The error rate performances being reported by Osnes states were beyond suspicious.

---

[12] (https://www.agri-pulse.com/articles/9168-states-fiddle-with-snap-error-rates-to-win-bonuses-from-usda).
[12b] (https://www.clarion-ledger.com/story/news/2017/11/29/doj-investigages-missippi-department-human-services-over-food-stamps-consultant/901927001/)

In 2013, Texas won a high performance bonus to the tune of $6,056,493 for having the lowest food stamp error rate. But again, like Florida, Texas has not been formally determined—as yet anyway—to be operating outside the allowable parameters of federal quality control guidelines. And also to be clear, I am not suggesting that the Texas chair of the House Agriculture Committee would in any way act duplicitously as he "monitors the investigation." I believe in trust until proven otherwise with only the reminder that it is decidedly every American's responsibility to watch over their government.

The scandal may have flown largely under the radar, but as of this writing, the Department of Justice continues to investigate states involved with Osnes: [12b]

> The U.S. Department of Justice is investigating Mississippi Department of Human Services over its management of the Supplemental Nutrition Assistance Program, formerly known as food stamps. Human Services is also the state agency expected to soon assume responsibility of Medicaid eligibility.
>
> The department first hired consultant Julie Osnes in 2011 to help improve its SNAP error rate, which, if low, can earn the state cash incentives. Federal investigators have discovered that through consultants like Osnes, states have manipulated their reported numbers, making them unreliable.
>
> Mississippi could have to pay back millions in bonuses it earned while using Osnes' services — at least $5.93 million between 2012 and 2015.

It is an identifying trait of fartworms that they do not play the long game.

Okay. Most all that you've just read is available for anyone who wants to swoggle through google results on the internet.[13]

Here's why it really matters.

Sure, the federal agency that runs the Food Stamp Program bungled unimaginably. (Well, "unimaginably" if you have zero imagination and blissfully no experience with self-interested fartworms in government.) But what has not been revealed as of this writing—is just how badly USDA's ineptness hurt honest States.

It works like this.

---

[13] Here's a good general overview: (http://origin-www.keloland.com/news/article/ investigates/sd-consultant-in-middle-of-federal-investigations-into-food-stamp-data-reporting-by-states)

As we've said, USDA provides millions in cash bonuses if they have among the lowest food stamp error rates. But the exact opposite is also true. USDA also charges financial penalties against states whose error rates are above the national average.

What?

Yeah. There is no hardline performance target for states. It moves from year to year. It's based on whatever the national average is for that year. Simply put, every year roughly half of states are below the national average and the other half of states are above the national average. Those above the average? The food stamp feds hit them with a sanction. If their rate is above the national average two years in a row, and is above 6%, they pay a cash penalty. Actually pay it.

The end result is this. States compete each year not just to win bonuses, but also to avoid paying federal cash penalties. Think about it. As a quality measure, it ludicrously assumes that half of all states each year are poor performers, as if it could never be possible that one year maybe 75% of States do a good job. Worse, it's a system that encourages each state to build quality strategies that, because it's a competitive environment, they can't share with other states. It's a system that promotes secrecy and corner-cutting because no Food Stamp Director wants to be the one going to his or her legislative Finance Committee to explain the sudden need for more general funds to pay a federal penalty, especially if they have to explain it's because of their own poor performance. It's a system that is in strident violation of practically every good outcome management principal.

Enter Osnes. She offered to take that stress away. Moreover, she operated for some fifteen years under the noses of the USDA Food and Nutrition Service.

And that's the problem.

The complicity of USDA Food and Nutrition Service is insidious. They simply looked the other way and that's difficult to prove. But they were very aware Osnes States were manipulating error numbers. In fact, for several years they told States not to embrace Osnes's strategies. But they directed no formal policies to stop them in States using them. Meanwhile we in New Hampshire continually waved the red flag in protest. But the food stamp feds in D.C. had a mammoth stake in keeping things quietly *status quo*. For one thing, that meant top USDA officials preened in front of Congress patting themselves on the back for what great integrity numbers they were putting up. That's always a good career move. And two, States the size of Florida carry tremendous political weight. Other huge States like California and Texas were also benefitting from the Osnes Miracle and receiving bonus money. What federal bureaucrat with career ambition is going to confront that kind of power in Congress?

But finally, in 2015, a whistle blower complained to the FBI. It took investigation by the Department of Justice's Office of Inspector General to force our federal fartworms at USDA to pay attention. USDA should have done the investigation. It took an outside entity to bring them into line.[14]

The whole scandal is like a fungus sucking the juice out of a rotting log, chaotic strands of it rooting and worming deep into the punky heartwood. USDA willingly screwed over smaller states—the ones who ran legitimate quality control in food stamps. How? Because when the Osnes States, who amounted to half the nation, began using steroids, they artificially lowered the national average error rate from 8.66 in 2001, about when Osnes became active, to 3.66 in 2014. In short, the half of states that used Osnes tactics competed for bonuses. The ones who didn't? They either performed spectacularly merely to survive without a penalty, or they wound up paying federal penalties to the feds, the penultimate insult from an uncaring federal system that hung them out to dry.

But what was most deeply disappointing to me personally was the behavior of trusted national organizations like the Center for Budget and Policy Priorities (CBPP) and the American Public Human Services Association (APHSA). These organizations purpose to advise States on welfare issues, to help them organize to have their issues presented in the national forum. They too knew of the hidden scandal. Non-Osnes states, like New Hampshire, raised concerns nationally, but to my knowledge not a peep made its way out of the national advocacy scene. I would hate to think it was because they needed the membership dues and continued support of large, powerful States like Florida, California, and Texas...despite that this came at the expense of smaller non-Osnes States. This might be understandable if it weren't that they went in the opposite direction to boast about the seemingly impeccable integrity of the food stamp program, I assume in hopes to shore up Congressional support for the program.[15] What makes this so deeply disappointing is that all my friends in those organizations have the deepest, soundest personal principals as appropriate for their calling. Yet small non-Osnes States were sacrificed.

In the end, now that the DOJ Office of Inspector General has ongoing investigations and has already found states guilty, a few Osnes States are beginning to pay back federal bonuses. Notably only the small ones so far.

What's the next step?

---

[14] https://www.usatoday.com/story/news/politics/2017/09/14/senate-panel-hears-manipulation-food-stamp-error-rates-seeks-improvements/666834001/)

[15] See (https://www.cbpp.org/research/snap-error-rates-at-all-time-lows)

Those states who had to pay federal penalties in those years for being over a discredited national average, should sue the USDA in a class action to recover penalty money. They would have a virtual lock on winning.

Meanwhile, maybe somebody should go to jail. Like the lead career administrator at the USDA Food and Nutrition Service in D.C.

Osnes States. This might be understandable if it weren't that they went in the opposite direction to boast about the seemingly impeccable integrity of the food stamp program, I assume in hopes to shore up Congressional support for the program.[14] What makes this so deeply disappointing is that all my friends in those organizations have the deepest, soundest personal principals as appropriate for their calling. Yet small non-Osnes States were sacrificed.

In the end, now that the DOJ Office of Inspector General has ongoing investigations and has already found states guilty, a few Osnes States are beginning to pay back federal bonuses. Notably only the small ones so far.

What's the next step?

Those states who had to pay federal penalties in those years for being over a discredited national average, should sue the USDA in a class action to recover penalty money. They would have a virtual lock on winning.

Meanwhile, maybe somebody should go to jail. Like the lead career administrator at the USDA Food and Nutrition Service in D.C.

CHAPTER 7

SNAP Drips with Gaudy Baubles

T he Food Stamp Program is riddled with policies that don't make any sense for the mission of the program or cost a bloated goatskin crammed with money. These are policies that produce no measurable results yet are protected by USDA officials and national advocates. This stubborn resistance to change by advocates is well-intended, for the fear is that one tiny slippage will bring about an avalanche of harm to low income people. I have supreme admiration for advocates. Federal officials in regional offices too. Food Stamp Officials in DC? Not so much.

But State bureaucrats are equally complicit. Suffice it to say that speaking out about the need for change caused the biggest doghouse I ever built myself to crawl into, complete with interior panels made of brightly colored broken shards of glass. It came about when I wrote a letter to Congress in spring of 2013 making food stamp recommendations for the Farm Bill being considered then. I didn't just send the letter, though. I obeyed protocol and sent it upstairs to an Associate Commissioner for approval and edits.

The crime?

Apparently I had impure thoughts. Here are the offending ideas:

> 1. High Performance Bonuses. Food Stamp recipients receive roughly $5.60 per day per person, not enough to feed them. Yet roughly $49 million a year is set aside to provide high performance bonuses to States for things like giving the right amount of benefits. Meanwhile, States who do poorly must pay cash penalties to the feds, making bonuses an expensive redundancy. Taxpayers are paying $49 million a year to fund no less than a proven corrupt quality control bonus system. I recommended eliminating high performance bonuses altogether.

I suspect most American taxpayers would agree that food stamp funding should go to feed low income people and not to bureaucrats doing their job.

> 2. Nutrition Education. Again, food Stamp recipients receive roughly $5.60 per day per person, not enough to feed them. Yet USDA spends $394 million a year to teach them how to eat properly (nutrition education). I don't disagree that wise food choices are critical to healthy living. Yet while nutrition education seems like a good idea to avoid childhood obesity and poor health, USDA has funded nutrition education for thirty years *yet has never required empiric data to show that it actually improved client eating behaviors long term.* Instead the measure was always about how many workshops were performed and where brochures were distributed. I recommended eliminating nutrition education, or at least making USDA demonstrate scientifically that the money paid for proven health outcomes.

Even more appropriately, it is long past due for Congress to seriously debate restricting food stamp purchases by eliminating client choice to buy sodas, potato chips, candies, gum, and such. Advocates call the food stamp program a "nutritional safety net." It's time to emphasize the "nutrition" part. This would also seem to be compatible with recent legislation restricting TANF cash from being used for liquor, gambling and adult entertainment, except in the case of food stamps such restrictions also bring the benefit of healthier diets and almost certain health cost savings in Medicare and Medicaid.

> 3. Employment and Training. Okay. Hear this one out. Food stamp employment and training is not what you think.

In 2013, USDA was spending $316 million on providing employment and training services to food stamp recipients. Should food stamp recipients be expected to go to work? Of course. But this is the rub: USDA once again manages by guesswork. USDA is spending that $316 million on employment and training while having never measured outcomes relative to how many people got jobs, retained jobs, attained job training, stayed off assistance, any of it. This is per the Government Accounting Office, "Multiple Employment and Training Programs: providing information on co-locating services and consolidating administrative structures could promote efficiencies," Appendix V, January 2011.

The sole study on the effectiveness of food stamp employment and training concluded:

> In the absence of employment and training, many of the individuals currently targeted by the program were able to

obtain similar referrals on their own. Consequently, it is not surprising, that employment and training was found to have no effect on participants' employment and earnings, and only a relatively small effect on average food stamp benefits. ("The National Evaluation of the Food Stamp Employment and Training Program," Journal of Policy Analysis and Management, Abstract, pages 311-330, vol 13, issue 2, Spring, 1994)

And there's more. Core federal policies in food stamp employment and training are dismissive of client accountabilities. For example, food stamp recipients are exempt from work requirements if they have a child under age six. For comparison, welfare reform in TANF exempts recipients for children under just age one. Even then, the TANF exemption is limited to just twelve months for the lifetime of the parent. Also, clients in food stamp employment and training are required to participate in work activities according to a formula: that is, they must do the number of hours a month determined by their food stamp allotment divided by the minimum wage. The average allotment in New Hampshire was $326, the minimum wages was $7.25, thus clients would average just ten hours a week. At a taxpayer cost of $316 million, does that make sense to you? Food Stamp Employment and Training is either a work program or it isn't.

My recommendation was simple. In 2009, the federal government spent $42 billion on a variety of independent employment and training programs across a multitude of agencies. Instead of building yet another employment and training program to be food stamp specific, let's be smart about it and simply require clients to demonstrate utilization of the employment opportunities under Wagner Peyser (unemployment offices) and the Workforce Opportunity Investment Act. They can get employment counseling there and we're already paying for those services. Meanwhile, the work requirement in food stamps would still have teeth. When Paul Ryan talks about consolidating programs in government, he's got the right idea.

4. Automatic Application for School Lunch. This one fries me. When an applicant for food stamps has children, USDA mandates that the names of the children be sent to local school districts so the children can be automatically determined eligible for School Lunch.

What's wrong with this? School lunch and kids, it's a no-brainer?
New Hampshire's experience was that food stamp families sometimes preferred to opt out of School Lunch for actually a pretty good reason. New Hampshire is a rural State and some clients would rather make a brown bag lunch for their children than endure having their small town, sometimes

chatty, school lunch person know their family receives food stamps. Until USDA forced us to change, New Hampshire sensibly allowed clients to choose whether their children's names were forwarded to schools. After all, nothing in the Food Stamp Act makes publicizing their participation by applying for School Lunch a condition of eligibility for food stamps. USDA argues that if a client wants to, they can decline School Lunch. A fartworm response because the problem here is they can decline only *after* their confidential food stamp information has been shared with the local school cafeteria supervisor. USDA officials pushed this policy because they were certain that School Lunch was good for you. Clients are, apparently, too stupid to make up their own minds.

This can be a problem among advocates. Do-gooders, who assume they know more about what's good for the people than the people themselves, are every bit as discriminatory as the people who put knee-jerk blame on people in poverty as being out-of-touch with God or inherently lazy.

My recommendation was to allow clients choice to decline School Lunch *before* their children's names were forwarded to the local school, *not after*.

When she read my ideas, the associate commissioner could very well have debated them with me. Or she could have edited. But instead she did what fartworms do. She grew angry instead of inventive. Opportunity was lost. Nothing changed.

But think about it. If just the first three items on this list had been adopted at the time I suggested them, no client would have been harmed yet the country would have seen about $3 billion in savings to date. Or better, that money could have been redirected to provide more food for hungry people which is, after all, the real mission of the program. The rest is just fluff. I know. $3 billion here. $3 billion there. Pretty soon you're talking real money.

But there's more. A new technology is available called "predictive analytics." What it is, is a computer algorithm that matches food stamp applicants with databases around the country to determine if the client is hiding wealth when they apply for food stamps. New Hampshire was one of the first states to look at making this a part of the application process. Before contracting with a company to provide this algorithm, I asked that they be paid based on a percentage of savings they brought to the state. I did this so that the contractor wouldn't just throw a ton of "hits" at us to work, when those hits had very little likelihood of panning out.

Here's the deal. State programs save state dollars. But food stamp savings save federal dollars. When I asked the USDA feds if they would be willing to pay a percentage of food stamp savings that would come back to them, they said "no."

No?

That was a death knell of the predictive analytics initiative in New Hampshire because the majority of savings to make it affordable for contractors was going to be food stamps, the biggest program. Since the feds refused to kick in, it was unaffordable for the State.

Tell me, what do you think about that? Fartworm food stamp feds in D.C. refuse to participate in an initiative to save taxpayer dollars?

As I said before, maybe someone there should go to jail.

In the end, now you know why they changed the name from the Food Stamp Program to the Supplemental Nutrition Assistance Program (SNAP). USDA in D.C. is incompetent at managing the program, so by calling it something else maybe it people would be distracted.

That would be called the *fartworm fix*.

CHAPTER 8

Where Does Humankind Find Common Ground? The Graveyard.

T he welfare debate has been with us seemingly forever yet some questions are so dicey they remain unresolved. For instance, does throwing the entire family off assistance because the adult won't participate in work activities motivate the adult to improve behavior, or does it unfairly punish the child? Should TANF parents be required to look for a job or participate in work activities before they are determined eligible for assistance? Is the 50% work participation the proper outcome measure for TANF? Should single parents on TANF be allowed to get Bachelor's Degrees paid for by welfare, knowing it will set them on a path to support their families, despite that at the same time other young college students who chose to wait to have children are racking up a lifetime of student loan debt which they'll pay back later while at the same time paying taxes toward the college tuition of those on welfare?

Regardless where you land on these questions, something has been missing in the debate, a piece that has the potential to help stars align toward consensus, at least to a degree.

When New Hampshire officials first built welfare work programs in 1996, they created weak penalties on clients who refused to engage. Why? Because they reasoned that reducing the family's benefits—especially cutting benefits off altogether—would harm the children in the case. And that does seem a reasonable sentiment—even noble, if you don't look closely.

Yet ironically, what was missing in New Hampshire's welfare debate then was precisely that we actually did *not* emphasize children.

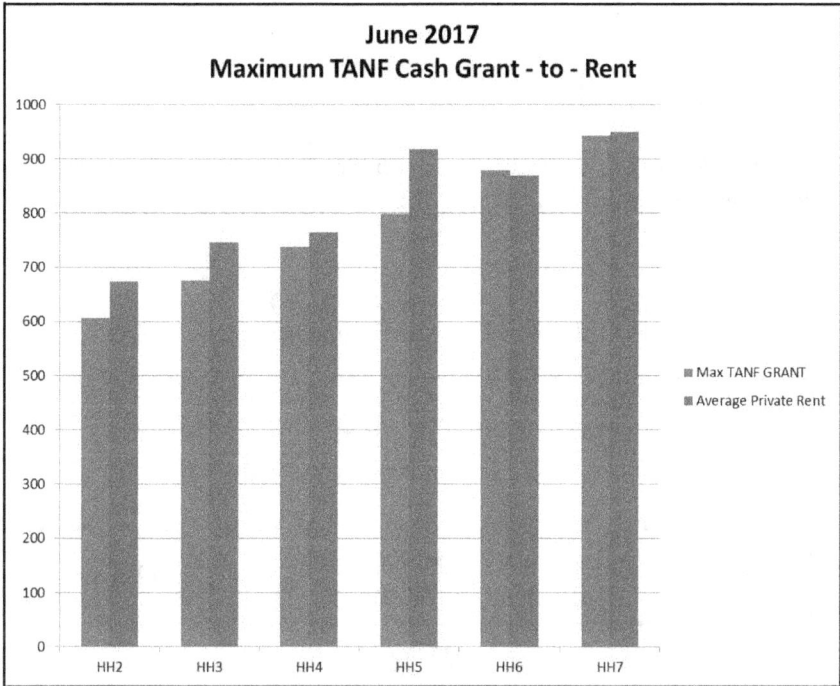

**June 2017
Maximum TANF Cash Grant - to - Rent**

Wait, you say. How can one side of the debate claim to be protecting children from harm, while the other side of the debate claims the same thing, that we would be protecting children? Who's right here?

Well, for starters, "emphasize the child" means that a well-managed welfare program must assess all policy choices looking at the long game and the child's place in it. That begins with asking the inconvenient question, *"What are the implications for children of simply being on TANF?"*

It's an odd omission, that question. It's a head-scratcher that until 2006 welfare administrators in New Hampshire had never thought to ask it. But when we did, we cast a sudden, glaring light on the ugly truth of welfare. The ugly truth is that welfare is a predatory trap. We are all of us its prey— Taxpayers, Republicans, Democrats, Independents, Recipients, Government, Advocates…everybody.

Just look at the chart below. Until June of 2017, *New Hampshire gave TANF clients about $75 less than what they were being charged for rent.* (HH means Household size). Landlords verify the amounts with us, so these are true numbers. Note: the rents welfare recipients were being charged were less than the State average for rents because the housing was substandard.

The ugly truth is that over five thousand welfare children began each month without enough assistance to pay rent and were already in danger of eviction. Now the desperation sets in: how to pay for life necessities.

Diapers? Heating? Electricity? Phone? Car? Gasoline? Tolls. Parking. Laundry. Bills for life necessities pour in, but there was not enough assistance income to secure even a roof over a TANF child's head.

That is unacceptable.

Data were clear. The safety net for children was broken. Every welfare child in New Hampshire was at risk of homelessness. Why? Because TANF cash grant levels are controlled by the legislature. But was it paying attention?

No.

It was carefully not looking.

This is the history of New Hampshire's grant level over a thirty year period, starting in 1987 when the grant level was 58% of federal poverty.

TANF GRANT LEVELS HISTORY

Effective Date	Parents and 3 Children	% Federal Poverty
July 1, 1987	$541.00	58%
July 1, 1988	$552.00	57%
July 1, 1989	$536.00	53%
July 1, 1990	$575.00	54%
July 1, 1991	$575.00	51%
July 1, 1992	$575.00	49%
July 1, 1993	$575.00	48%
July 1, 1994	$613.00	50%
July 1. 1995	$613.00	49%
July 1, 1996	$613.00	47%
January 1, 1997	$613.00	46%
July 1, 1998	$613.00	45%

August 1, 1999	$639.00	46%
April 1, 2000	$663.00	47%
July 1, 2001	$663.00	45%
July 1, 2002	$688.00	46%
July 1, 2003	$688.00	45%
July 1, 2004	$688.00	44%
July 1, 2005	$688.00	43%
July 1, 2006	$688.00	41%
July 1, 2007	$688.00	40%
August 1, 2008	$738.00	42%
August 1, 2009	$738.00	40%
August 1, 2010	$738.00	40%
August 1, 2011	$738.00	40%
August 1, 2012	$738.00	38%
August 1, 2013	$738.00	38%
August 1, 2014	$738.00	37%
August 1, 2015	$738.00	37%
August 1, 2016	$738.00	36%
March 1, 2017	$738.00	36%

In 1987, the TANF grant level was at 58% of federal poverty. Thirty years later it represented 36% of federal poverty.

Over the course of thirty years the TANF grant increased by $197 per month, or 36%. However inflation over this same time period was 114%. (Inflationdata.com). Poverty is considered "deep" when it is under 50% of the federal poverty line. By 2017 New Hampshire provided a welfare grant well under the deep poverty line. But was New Hampshire the worst in the nation?

Nope.

Not even close. Until 2017, New Hampshire actually had about the nation's 6th highest cash assistance level for children.

So what about the other benefits like food stamps? Don't they help?

Yes. Of course they do. But not like you might think. For one thing, food stamps can only be spent on food. They can't help pay for rent, utilities, clothes, diapers, transportation, heating … So for a TANF mother facing eviction and the prospect of living in her car with her children, America might want to think twice about condemning her for selling her food stamps so she can make up that $75 needed for rent to keep a roof over her kids' heads.

Second, the general public seems pretty unclear about this, so let's just put it out there. *Food stamps do not cover the full cost of food.* The maximum food stamp allotment nationwide is $5.60 per person per day. It was never intended to meet the full food needs of recipients. But TANF recipients don't receive this maximum food stamp allotment because SNAP allotments are reduced by any income—including the TANF cash grant—by a factor of roughly $1 for every $3 in TANF income. This is because food stamp law assumes TANF cash assistance can help supplement a family's food needs. That assumption is…ridiculous. When Congress developed food stamp law, they either weren't informed on the issue or chose to look away.

What about other programs of assistance, such as the Child Care Program? It is true that the intent of Welfare Reform was that each able-bodied welfare recipient be engaged in work activities. The Child Care Subsidy Program was developed alongside TANF to assist with that. Welfare mothers must have child care so they have a safe place to leave their children while they report to employment activities. Problem solved, right?

Uhm…not entirely.

See, even though it's a program designed to pay for child care for low income workers, fartworm rules were built into the program to make welfare clients pay a "cost share," that is a percentage of their income. In New Hampshire, that share is 4% of their income. But again, if the TANF cash assistance grant already doesn't cover rent, and food stamps don't cover the cost of food, how then is it to be expected that another 4% of the TANF benefit must be earmarked for child care? Clearly when Congress adopted child care law, they either weren't informed on the issue, or they chose to look away.

Oh well, at least there's housing assistance, right? Housing assistance? Most TANF clients get help with housing, right?

Wrong.

In New Hampshire, there's an eight year wait list to get subsidized housing. Only 8% of TANF recipients receive it.[16]

So where does all this lead us?

A growing body of research has highlighted the crucial nature of children's brain development during their most formative 0-5 years. Jack Shonkoff, M.D. (*The Science of Early Childhood Development: Closing the Gap between What We Know and What We Do*), describes long-term damage to children from living in poverty, damage that is neurological in nature and that becomes more permanent the longer the child is in poverty. Shonkoff's research, along with others, has brought the importance of brain development in relation to poverty to the attention of the American public.

So this is the ugly truth about welfare that never makes headlines. The TANF cash safety net for children is so inadequate it leaves children not just in poverty, but *deep* poverty. The TANF experience is nothing less than a ticking time bomb for children receiving assistance. The longer kids are on TANF—the longer they are in deep poverty—the more neurological damage can incur. And when they become poorly functioning adults as a result, what then?

Where does this leave the debate?

The inconvenient question was, *"What are the implications for children of simply being on TANF?"* It had an obvious answer. As a welfare administrator, clearly any policy that extended a child's time on TANF, was harmful to that child. Unless States have the political will to provide an adequate cash safety net for children—which is unlikely—then the only choice is to move those children out of poverty through the employment of their parents, and not delay in doing it. Today's approach to administering welfare must begin with considering exactly where and how children on assistance are being cared for during their early years.

So much for allowing welfare adults six months of welfare while refusing to go to work activities because shutting them off benefits would be cruel to the children.

Or as my favorite commissioner quite adroitly put it, "TANF is simply not good enough for children."

Here's a not-so-obvious impact on kids.

I once asked a group of TANF clients about the worst implications of poverty on their children. One said, *"Believe it or not, a lacrosse stick. My son wants one, but they cost $149. Where am I going to get $149 so my child can play lacrosse?"*

She was right. Sports in schools cost money. But sports and band—and other outside activities in school—bond children **TO school**. Impoverished kids who cannot afford to participate are segregated **FROM school**. That's

---

[16] Makes sense. The average time on TANF is only eighteen months, give or take a week or two. Clients aren't on assistance long enough to get past the eight year waiting period for housing assistance.

not to say that schools aren't great about providing free equipment where they can. But have any of you ever had to use that crappy community baseball mitt from the team's equipment bag? In any case, overall, what are the obvious educational implications for kids?

Consequences of the TANF cash size are very real-life. One of our clients needed a place to live and couldn't find anything she could afford, so brought her children to live with a 70 year old man. Later she reported to her welfare employment counselor that she was blacking out at night and waking up bleeding. ...We discovered the older man was drugging her, then abusing her.

The end result is this. Regardless which side of the aisle your political sentiments rest with—Republican or Democrat or Independent—your welfare system in American is the quintessential gaudy bauble, a piece of bright political paste jewelry designed to falsely awe and impress the public.

Everyone is cheated here. The American myth we're all tugged into believing is that we Americans take good care of our poor children. We opt in to the hype that we are a country of superior morals with the ethical credentials to criticize other countries for their human rights violations. After all, those countries allow child labor, right?

But the American truth is itself inconveniently ugly. Statues of Charles Dickens are frowning in embarrassment at us. American babies are living in cars while legislatures in nearly every state are squandering TANF money that's supposed to go to help them.

In fact, in 2015 only 25% of mandatory TANF spending went to actual safety net services.[17] The rest of the money earmarked by federal law was diverted by States to other budget needs.

What are we to do?

For starters, improvement is possible. In New Hampshire, I made several attempts to increase the TANF grant so it could meet at least some of a family's life essentials, including rent. The first attempt in 2006 led to creation of a bipartisan legislative study committee to review the adequacy of the TANF grant. That committee looked at inflation figures, cost of housing, cost of child care, cost of food, and more. I represented the Department on that Committee. We came up with some proposals, one of which was to increase the TANF grant.

Then go figure.

One of the Advocates who served on the Committee was tapped to testify to the legislature on our findings. We sat side-by -side and suddenly the Advocate said something entirely different. He told the Committee we didn't need a TANF grant increase because we could simply adjust how we deducted rent costs from income. He had apparently gone to someone he

---

[17] (https://www.cbpp.org/blog/examining-tanf-in-brief)

thought knew better than the committee he'd just served on, and got bad information. See, not everyone on TANF has income to deduct the rent from. And what about homeless people on welfare who are unable to scrape together enough money to pay a deposit on an apartment? To this day I have no idea how a respected advocate like him could betray so many colleagues that sat with him on the study Committee. In the enthralled grips of his own ego, he thought he knew better, which is just one more way the stars can fail to align and welfare can fail to meet its mission.

The harm was done. The legislature took no action. Probably they wouldn't have anyway.

Thenceforth, every second year during budget sessions I presented requests to increase the TANF grant. Yet even with a Democrat House, Democrat Senate and Democrat Governor, only a few courageous members of the legislature like Mary Jane Wallner had political courage. The rest shrank from looking weak on welfare. For instance, when I put the request in my budget yet again, the leader of a Democratic Governor's budget team allegedly said, "No. Those people don't vote." The request to right-size the TANF grant didn't even make it to the legislature. Welfare grant adjustments went nowhere despite the fact that the Department twice had been accruing $40 to $70 million in unspent federal TANF dollars earmarked for specifically TANF. The State's treasury wasn't the problem here.

Then in the 2018/2019 budget request I changed tactics.

This time instead of putting a TANF grant increase into the budget, I phrased legislative language to "link the TANF grant to 60% of federal poverty and tie it to inflation annually." It sailed through a Republican House, Republican Senate, and Republican Governor and became effective July 1, 2017.

What? *Why?*

Political parties aren't the issue here. Many more stars than that have to align. According to some of my friends in the legislature—and I have good ones on both sides of the aisle—they passed the budget with the grant increase because the less discriminating legislators—potentially the ones with knee-jerk objections—didn't understand what "60% of poverty" meant. But then no one did. At the time even advocates were calling my friends at New Hampshire Legal Assistance to ask why was the Department "reducing" the TANF grant. Apparently nobody—even after all the educating I had tried over the years— understood that 60% of poverty was in reality an increase from the then-current cash grant that was sized at 36% of poverty.

Later, after the budget passed, questions started rising about why the TANF caseload was trending up. I was asked to respond to those questions by drafting a letter that was sent to the chairs of Senate and House Finance Committees in November 2017. It began like this:

This letter is to respond to questions the Department has received from legislators about the TANF caseload. Per the TANF Snapshot Report for the end of October, the TANF cash program grew by 1279 individuals since July 1, 2017. Children comprised 918 of this growth (72%), adults 361. Of adults, 307 of 361 (85%) are in the NH Employment Program and verified as meeting mandatory work requirements each week. Not in work programs, 45 adults have disabilities whom the Department will be facilitating toward federal disability cash programs. The TANF caseload is right-sizing as a result of linking the TANF grant to 60% of federal poverty, allowing the Department to work with more parents to move their children out of poverty through employment.

In the end, it may be true that legislators didn't know what they were passing when they approved a budget linking TANF to 60% of poverty. But it is also true that emotional, ideological and political limits had always prevented them from engaging in any discussion deep enough on the issue of right-sizing welfare payments to achieve a real understanding of it. The result is that as of this writing no law has been drafted to repeal the grant increase. I suspect the reality may be that the change flew so far under the radar, legislators on both sides of the aisle who maybe wanted to do the right thing finally had the political cover to do so, and others finally understood the issue better. Or it could be that the legislature doesn't want to repeal the increase because then they have to go on record as putting children at risk of homelessness again, something they did invisibly before. In any case, the stars have finally aligned for public policy to progress. There was a personal political price to be paid, though, and I paid it. Make no mistake: I'd pay it again.

Has the safety net in New Hampshire, at least, been salvaged?

Maybe. Kind of. Sorta.

The TANF grant level in New Hampshire is no longer "deep poverty." But it is only ten points above it. To show how deeply rooted the issue is, children remain nevertheless at risk. The chart below describes how the old grant (in gray at 36% of poverty) and the new grant (in green at 60% of poverty) stack up against life necessities as studied by MIT. Data are as of December 2017.

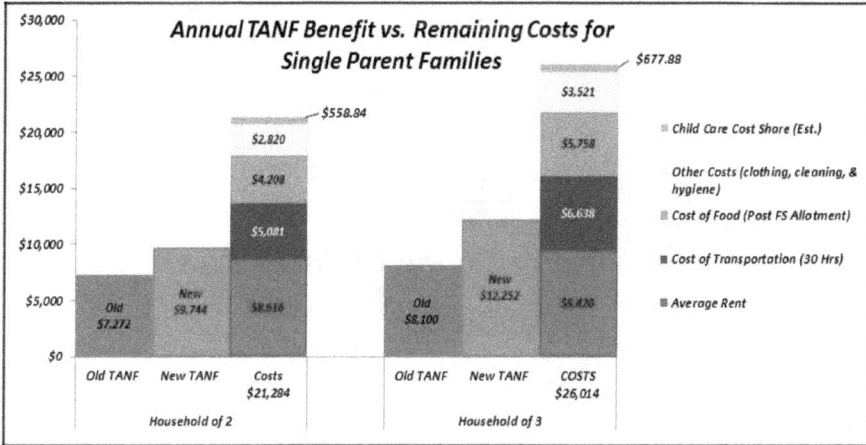

Annual TANF Benefit vs. Remaining Costs for Single Parent Families

Legend:
- Child Care Cost Share (Est.)
- Other Costs (clothing, cleaning, & hygiene)
- Cost of Food (Post FS Allotment)
- Cost of Transportation (30 Hrs)
- Average Rent

Household of 2:
- Old TANF $7,272
- New TANF $9,744
- Costs $21,284: $558.84 / $2,820 / $4,208 / $5,081 / $8,616

Household of 3:
- Old TANF $8,100
- New TANF $12,252
- COSTS $26,014: $677.88 / $3,521 / $5,758 / $6,638 / $8,420

Source: http://livingwage.mit.edu/states/33

What lesson can we take away about America's "safety net"?

We learn that across the nation the American safety net is an old cobweb sagging in filmy gray tatters from the crystal chandeliers of Congress. As a net, it catches dust and maybe a mite or two.

Can the debate reach some compromise before we all of us age our way into the common ground of the graveyard?

Yes. It can. We did it in New Hampshire. More needs to be done, but policy has progressed. TANF recipients are now accountable to move their children out of poverty through work, but now also they can afford to be on the program while they do it.

CHAPTER 9

But Tell Me, Where Do the Children Play?

– Cat Stevens

I hope we can agree by now that TANF Program has two missions. First, it's a cash safety net for low income children. Second, it's to move those children out of poverty through employment of their parents. How does the Child Care Program fit?

As a condition of eligibility every able -bodied TANF mother has a twenty or thirty hour a week work requirement. So while she works, any child in the house under age thirteen needs child care. For that reason, Congress developed the Child Care Subsidy Program as a supplement to TANF. Under the Child Care Program the State pays for child care while mom is participating in work activities.

Job done. Right? Mom can go to work and the kids are safe?

Alas, a nagging statistic needed explaining. Data consistently show just 26% of New Hampshire TANF clients use the Child Care Subsidy Program despite being mandatory for work programs.

That never made sense, so to confirm I asked for a series of specialized reports. When data came back, we adjusted it to remove recipients from it who were exempt from the work requirement—such as for having a child less than one year of age. Even after the adjustments, the usage of the child care program adjusted upwards to just 34%. What did that mean?

66%—or two-thirds—of the caseload with a child thirteen or younger were *not* using the New Hampshire Child Care Subsidy Program.

How can that make sense? TANF moms must participate in work activities for twenty to thirty hours a week. They need child care for their children. The State has a program to pay for Child Care. But TANF moms weren't using it. Why? And just where the heck were those children? Were they in quality care? Were they even safe?

In 2005, we set about determining what barriers might exist to child care participation by posing a set of questions that would answer

> 1) what was the out-of-pocket cost of licensed child care centers charged to TANF families? And
> 2) what type of child care were TANF parents using? Clearly, if two-thirds of TANF parents were not utilizing the scholarship to access regulated child care— that is, child care that is state-inspected and hence likely safer—then exactly where *were* TANF parents leaving their kids?

Some history first.

Prior to 2004, the general assumption was that New Hampshire's Child Care Program met the full cost of child care for a TANF family. Then in 2005 as the new Director of the Division of Family Assistance (DFA), the division in charge of the TANF Program, I was embarking my agency on an evidence-based management model. I had hired an amazing child care expert on staff, and one of the first scientific evaluations she conducted for us was a survey of child care providers.

The results of her survey were frightening.

Not only did TANF parents receiving help through the Child Care Subsidy Program experience out-of-pocket costs, but these costs actually made regulated child care unaffordable.

That was an eye-opener.

That was also when in a separate, but related, analysis we assessed the TANF cash grant in relation to cost of rent and found that the grant was consistently less than the rent landlords certify they owe. Later, that rental deficit grew to as much as $75. The conclusion was revelatory. Since TANF clients could not afford rent, clearly any out-of-pocket expense beyond that was also unaffordable.

How much in out-of-pocket expenses were TANF clients paying for child care, even when the Child Care Subsidy Program was supposedly taking care of their child care needs? Our child care expert's data indicated that 78% of child care providers charged clients a co-payment over and above what the State would reimburse for child care. That meant the TANF client paid the difference out-of-pocket. The average cost was $77 per month per child.

Then things changed ... but didn't get better. Not long after our study, the Child Care feds swooped in and told New Hampshire we had to come more into compliance with certain federal requirements. So in 2009 New

Hampshire's Child Care Program implemented changes to do this. As a result, in 2013 I asked our child care expert to once again study child care costs to TANF parents. This time she did a survey of 64 centers representing 143 early childhood and school-age program sites.

Data came back showing that New Hampshire's new 2009 Child Care Program redesign shuffled provider reimbursement rates and client out-of-pocket expenses, but ultimately afforded TANF recipients no net financial relief. Remember, the previous 2005 survey showed clients paid an out-of-pocket average $77 per child per month for costs associated with State reimbursements that failed to cover provider rates. This new 2013 survey showed co-payments *per se* were no longer so bad but still posed a problem. (Again, co-payments are the difference between what the State reimburses and what the child care center charges.)

But while co-payments themselves were not as high since the 2009 redesign, other expenses had taken their place.

Before 2005, TANF clients in New Hampshire paid a token couple of dollars for "cost share." (Cost share is the federally mandated skin-in-the-game that Congress requires of child care program recipients.) The child care feds told New Hampshire that our cost share was too low, so we raised it.[18] Our 2013 data showed TANF recipients in New Hampshire were now paying $22.52 per month in cost share. Also, although not considered true "co-payments," most providers (79.69%) charged additional fees for activities, transportation, or late pickup. Another 45.31% of providers charged TANF families the first week's fee before they begin services for the child.

But the costliest of the new child care out-of-pocket expenses to TANF clients was something called the *"service level drop."*

What is that? It's an industry standard that child care providers charge parents for days when a child does not go to the child care provider for care. It doesn't matter whether the absence is due to sickness of the child or parent, or even whether absence is due to the center's own closing for holiday or vacation. The Center still charges for the child.

That's where the issue comes in.

New Hampshire's Child Care Subsidy Program would reimburse providers for absentee charges...until total absences in the week caused the service

---

[18] Is the theme of ignorance clear by now? The federal agency that heads TANF is the US Department of Health and Human Services, Administration for Children and Families. That same federal agency heads the Child Care Subsidy Program. If anybody should have known that the TANF cash assistance level couldn't survive additional costs, it was they. Oh well. Without fartworms, there wouldn't be this book.

level to drop from full-time reimbursement rates to half-time rates, or half-time to part-time.[19] Then the TANF parent had to pay the difference. I won't get into the minutiae of policy here. Suffice it to say that service level drops caused an out-of-pocket expense to Child Care Program recipients 34% of the time, or in other words once every three weeks. Charges ranged from $38 to $78 per week per child.

In the end, cumulative out-of-pocket costs to TANF recipients were s ubject to more variables than they were in 2005 when we did our first study. But TANF cash grants still did not cover the cost of rent and child care out-of-pocket expenses remained about $75 per month.

So no big surprise. 66% of TANF mothers continued to avoid the Child Care Program. And it wasn't just TANF parents who were priced out of regulated child care. TANF leavers were also. Among TANF parents who left cash assistance for employment over a recent four year period, 39% of them recidivated back onto TANF citing the unaffordability of child care as a contributing factor.

So did Congress act? Did they bring out their plumbers toolbox and set about wrenching this cost share policy back from lunacy?

Nope.

They did change the Child Care Program again, though. But rather than make child care affordable so welfare moms could get to work, Congress took the "We know what's best for you route" and bungled badly in two ways. One, they enacted a law that put mandates on States to add new quality measures on child care. That meant States needed to promote early learning by moving child care providers toward low child/teacher ratios, hiring staff with more education, meeting higher accreditation standards, and so on. That in and of itself isn't bad. Good for kids to have better quality care, right?

But Congress provided zero new money to implement these changes. That meant States had to take money away from existing child care programs to meet these new federal requirements. That meant either one of two things. One, reduce the child care reimbursement rates to providers, making welfare moms pay even more in co-pay. Or two, limit the pool of people eligible for the Child Care Program by creating a waitlist, so low-income people who need help with child care get zero help until their name comes up…if they can keep their job that long.

So tell me, where do the children play?

If not in regulated child care, where are they? Priced out of regulated child care, most TANF parents turn to free child care from friends, neighbors, boyfriends or family, that is if they're not sending latchkey kids home alone.

---

[19] As you would expect, the Child Care Subsidy Program gives parents full time rates when they work full time and need day long care. Half-time and part-time are for those who need less child care.

At this point in the writing of this book, I started doing research on the likelihood of mom's boyfriends and other non-relatives assaulting toddlers. I was going to give you some examples of several children who were murdered by mom's boyfriend right here in New Hampshire over the past few years…New Hampshire which is perennially ranked as one of the best states in in the country to raise children. I was going to talk about one TANF mom who we counseled for domestic violence, who did everything right, who went through our work training program, and who was on her first day on the job, when her boyfriend who was babysitting fist- punched her two year old toddler multiple times in the stomach and killed him. Mom didn't even make it to lunch time. I was going to give you all that, and maybe mention the Commissioner covered up that my division had predicted something like that and prepared a prevention plan the year before but couldn't get it approved. But then I basically couldn't. Assaults on children are a precipice I don't think I could survive the leap from.

You'll have to look it all up on your own.

In the end, in their most recent child care legislation, Congress insisted State child care programs promote quality, then made it so low-income children were priced out of access to that quality child care. Isn't there anybody at the federal level who can put it all together?

This meets all the criteria of a gaudy bauble. Congress gets to look like they're on the moral high ground helping children get "quality" care yet at the same time they don't have to spend a dime on it. Early Learning advocates who advised them during the lawmaking get a bigger slice of the program pie to implement quality measures. Taxpayers avoid having to pay more taxes. And the children, kids in deep poverty who more than any others need safe, quality care? They get screwed. And sometimes they get dead.

Does anybody besides me have a problem with this?

CHAPTER 10

The ABC's of EBT: Just What Are Clients Buying with Their Benefits?

T he least understood term in welfare is "Electronic Benefits Transfer," or EBT. People call it a program. It's not. Or they imbue it with some sparkly magic that it just can't do. I'll explain that in a minute.

EBT has just one job. It is a debit card that carries food stamp and cash benefits. Food Stamps may only be used for food. Cash can be used at stores and ATM's. EBT is not a credit card. It can't be used over the internet. It's a debit card only.

Yet for all its simplicity of purpose, politically speaking EBT is a leaky drum of hi-test gasoline at the center of the fiery debate that always surrounds welfare.

Some background.

Until the late 1990's food stamps in New Hampshire were delivered to clients in the form of paper coupons (see Appendix A for more on this). Coupons were the same as cash except they could only be used in stores that certified with the USDA as food stamp retailers. Clients did not need to show personal identification to spend coupons. More on this in a minute.

Food Stamp Stuffing Day. During the over quarter century I was with the Department of Health and Human Services, food stamps were delivered on the 5th of the month. In the beginning, it worked like this. In the basement at 6 Hazen Drive in Concord, the Department maintained—and I believe still has—a secure vault that would be the envy of many local banks. In this vault, was stored New Hampshire's supply of food stamp coupons. Meanwhile, on the third floor of the building was the Department's Bureau of Data Management. Back then it was a pool of twenty-six or so clerical workers in a vast open work area. No cubicles in those days.

On the 5th of each month, food stamp stuffing day happened, where the clerical workers in the Bureau of Data Management put aside their normal work and cleared everything off their desks. When all was tidy, two uniformed security guards accompanied workers from the vault pushing tall rolling trays of that month's paper food stamp coupons into the room. Allocations of food stamp booklets were stacked on worker desks according to the denominations, accompanied by mailing envelopes and that worker's list of clients and the amount of food stamps each was supposed to receive that month.

New Hampshire clerical workers hand-stuffed as many as 23,000 envelopes on Stuffing Day. Then each worker handed each envelope off to another worker to be counted again for accuracy. I was the Food Stamp Program Manager back then. I made it my responsibility to buy two dozen donuts for this room of people every few months. (I sometimes wondered if any food stamp recipients were curious how cruller crumbs wound up in their food stamp envelopes....) When all envelopes were stuffed, they were loaded back into the rolling trays and delivered to the US Post Office for delivery to clients.

So far, it's an unimpeachable process. Security was impeccable. So what exactly comes next?

First, remember that coupons were like cash in a supermarket. People could use them with no ID, so anyone stealing them would be, in essence, stealing greenbacks, though they could only be spent on food. Second, Food Stamp Stuffing Day happened on the same day each month, so there was predictable notice when food stamps would be hitting the mail. Third, food stamps were just that, hitting the mail, which means they were being left in client mail boxes where any thief could pluck them out. Fourth—and my favorite—the US Postal Service didn't have anywhere near the Department's food stamp security. In fact, once they collected the trays upon trays of food stamps, their version of security was to take those trays of food stamps to their Manchester center of operations and leave them unattended in the middle of a warehouse with all the other mail.

In the 1990's, I was New Hampshire's Food Stamp Program Manager responsible for tracking food stamp mail loss. It averaged $8,000 a month. There were rules about how often a client could request replacement of lost/ stolen benefits, but in the end there were almost no real management controls to ensure that benefits had actually been lost as opposed to fraudulently being claimed. What I do know is that I worked closely with US Postal Inspectors who would, time to time, watch the Manchester warehouse floor through spy holes in the ceiling. Over a three or four year period, they caught two postal workers shoplifting food stamp envelopes from the trays. A third postal worker was investigated and his house was searched. Inspectors found undelivered mail and food stamps in the worker's house.

Food stamp coupons were inefficient in myriad other ways. USDA had to maintain an operation to print coupons similar to the process that the US Treasury had to print paper money. Then coupons had to be sorted into appropriate denominations that coincided with each State's food stamp caseload. Then the coupons had to be bundled and shipped securely to each state across the country. On delivery, each shipment had to be counted and ownership transferred with signatures for delivery and acceptance. Federal regulations required each State to have secure storage—hence the safe at our Hazen Drive facility. Coupons were required to undergo monthly inventories by multiple staff. Then each month during food stamp stuffing day, coupons were hand counted according to a master list of clients. Costs also included the price of mailing a packet of coupons to each client. And, on the back end, participating retailers accepted coupons from clients shopping in their grocery stores, then needed a separate process from cash and checks to redeem those coupons for US currency. USDA completed the process by reconciling used food stamp coupons against issued coupons and State inventory reports, then destroyed the coupons in a secure environment. Clearly there was room for much more efficiency.

Enter EBT.

In 1997, I got to be a part of something new. All Northeastern states decided to work together to contract for a new benefit delivery system: EBT. We called it The Northeastern Consortium of States and it included Maine, New Hampshire, Connecticut, Vermont, Massachusetts, Rhode Island, and New York. A consortium of this type was advantageous because EBT contractors based their pricing on the number of food stamp and cash cases—and New York brought plenty of those to the table. As an example, at the time New Hampshire had about 23,000 food stamp cases. New York had about 990,000. Sponsored by the USDA, the EBT initiative piggybacked on the commonly used existing infrastructure for commercial debit and credit cards.

EBT profoundly lowered the cost to deliver not just food stamp benefits, but also cash. In the decades before 1997, all cash benefits were mailed to recipients as bank checks twice a month, on the 15th and the 31st. Estimated costs were between $ 5.00 and $15.00 or higher per check for printing, mailing, replacing lost checks, reconciling checks, and so on...twice a month. EBT, on the other hand, reduced the cost to just 77 cents per case per month.

There's more.

Once we had sent a check and a recipient cashed it, that money was lost to the State financial system. Under EBT, though, clients spent money out of a state business account, which means any unused portion of the cash benefits returns to the State after 90 days of account inactivity, a savings to New Hampshire of about $130,000 per year. Happily, this amount is roughly the total annual cost to New Hampshire to issue cash via EBT, making cash issuance via EBT effectively free. Under EBT, cash benefits are automatically electronically available to the client's EBT account twice a month. Recipients may access cash through either direct purchase, ATM withdrawal, or cash-back at a Point of Sale device during retail purchases.

Food stamps are different. Under the old food stamp coupon system, as we've seen, food stamp coupons were cashable by anyone possessing them, and reports of lost or stolen coupons came in each month to the tune of about $8,000. Under EBT, though, reports of theft of benefits dropped to near zero.

When benefits became electronic, they could no longer be lost or stolen in the mail. Access to EBT benefits is secured via a Personal Identification Number (PIN) known only to the recipient, unless the recipient chooses to share it, same as for any bank debit card. Thus a client may no longer claim stolen benefits because even if somebody stole their card, they couldn't access benefits without also having the PIN.

We should note, though, that EBT did not also solve food stamp trafficking. Clients who sold food stamp coupons on the street for fifty cents on the dollar, can still sell use of their card or even more invisibly still make purchases with food stamps and sell the purchases for fifty cents on the dollar. And fraudulent store owners can still swipe a card and give the money to the recipient while taking a 50% "fee" for themselves. Often they're only caught because they make repetitive even-dollar "purchases," which is the same as them suspiciously telling USDA that this same client came in three times in a ten minute period and each time bought exactly $100 in groceries.

As Food Stamp Program Manager then, I got to be New Hampshire's first EBT expert. In all, I spent about eighteen months in the late 1990's traveling to and from Albany, New York for EBT meetings to work out how EBT would function. Because we in the Northeast were at the forefront of EBT, we had a number of interesting issues to deal with for the first time. For instance, if a food stamp client was leaving the Northeast and moving to a state that didn't have EBT yet—and most didn't—how would we deal with their food stamp benefits. EBT food stamps required a special point of sale device in a store. Obviously, then, clients couldn't use EBT in States where EBT had not yet arrived in stores. To complicate matters, States with EBT no longer had food stamp coupons—I mean, that was the whole point—so we couldn't just give clients food stamp coupons to take with them when they moved out of state. Meanwhile, USDA was decidedly not in favor of cashing out a client's food stamps so they could use cash money to shop for food when they arrived at their destination.

As a solution one USDA representative in an Albany meeting said, "Why don't we just require they buy all their groceries before they move?" The federal guy who said that was actually pretty competent, but it just goes to show that everyone can be a fartworm sometimes. I asked him to think about it. "Imagine you've got your family all packed up with everything you own in a car and a U-Haul trailer. You're moving out of state. Now you're going to stop at the grocery store, buy several hundred dollars' worth of groceries, and find niches and crannies among the furniture to cram it in? Meanwhile you've got no refrigerator for milk and eggs?" Ultimately, though, these kinds of issues dissipated because within a few years EBT was universal across the country. Each state was required to accept a universal EBT technology. USDA called this "interstate interoperability."

And then the trouble started.

In May of 2012, a clerk in a small store in, as it happens, the tiny town of Peterborough, New Hampshire, made national headlines. Why? Because a young man came into her store and tried to buy a pack of cigarettes with the cash benefits on his EBT card. The clerk refused to sell it to him and in the process became a national hero of sorts and the center of a media firestorm. And because the public focused so vividly on it, some politicians came out of the woodwork to share in the limelight.

That one incident in Peterborough led to much in the way of indignant scrutiny. For instance, our local New Hampshire news station, WMUR Channel 9, advertised they would be building an expose on how EBT was being mis-used. New Hampshire's Speaker of the House held a press conference on the issue (but excluded the Concord Monitor, our capitol's newspaper, because of some feud he had going with them). The Legislative Audit Team was assigned to review EBT. And a bill was introduced in the legislature to restrict purchases using EBT. The bill led to a study committee. As Director of the Division that was in charge of EBT, this was all served up to me for response like a steaming poop pie.

So what exactly was/is the debate? You likely already have your opinion, but let's break it down. First, I think there's general agreement in America that welfare is necessary to give people a hand up, not hand out. Benefits are meant to help people with life essentials.

After that, it all sort of goes haywire.

First, what exactly is a "life necessity"? Who is responsible for determining what is and what is not necessary for a family's life? How can EBT stop welfare recipients from buying things that are not "life necessities"? Should EBT be allowed for use out-of-state? Why does government give cash at all? Why not just pay landlords directly for rent, electric companies for utilities, and so on? Then, couldn't we restrict how much a client could withdraw at an ATM? Should a photo be put on the card to ensure someone isn't using it fraudulently?

Let's try to break some of this out.

One of the first things to happen was that our local news station, WMUR, on August 2, 2012 ran a story they advertised as an expose claiming that "More than $90,000 in five months was spent or withdrawn from New

Hampshire EBT cards in 35 other states. That represents about 2.3 percent of the total money spent using EBT cards over the time period." ("Records Show Questionable Use of EBT Cards") It is worth noting, however, that $67,000 of the $ 90,000 spent out-of-state, was spent in border states where clients may likely go to find better prices. That means just 6/10ths of one percent were spent in non-border states.

There's one more piece of this that we must remind ourselves about. Welfare cash isn't just TANF for single parents. It also includes cash programs for the disabled, the blind and the elderly for whom graduation into employment isn't an expectation. Moreover, when the disability is severe enough—especially when it's a mental disability—the person who actually uses the EBT card may be acting on behalf of a family member. Such a caregiver is called a "caretaker relative." At one point during this long debate in New Hampshire, someone drew attention to the fact that an EBT card was being used in Puerto Rico. Turns out that the individual on benefits was severely disabled and had accompanied his parents—his caregivers—to visit relatives in Puerto Rico. In other cases, elderly clients on Old Age Assistance went to visit family for a week or two in Florida during the winter. Are these things bad?

Nothing in welfare debates is quite as black-and-white as we'd like it to be.

What I still laugh about to this day, is WMUR's crew when they came to interview me. The station sent a reporter and a television camera man to my office. Almost immediately it was clear the reporter intended to get me on record admitting to being responsible for misuse of EBT across state lines. "What should you have done to stop that from happening?" the reporter asked, not just once, but several times in several different ways. I responded that my job as government was to implement law and that there was no law restricting where EBT can be used. After a couple of go-rounds like this, he asked me yet again. This time I was losing patience. "Tell you what," I said. "Let's you and I go down to your car right now. I'm going to require you to pop the trunk and if I see anything inside that I don't like (say, a grimy tire iron), I'm going to take you to the police station and charge you. I'm government, I can do that, right?" The reporter's camera man laughed quietly. Then I added, "No, I can't do that, can I. There is no law that tells me to do that and I can't make up my own laws. It's the same with people using EBT out-of-state. They are breaking no law and I have no authority to go after them." In the end, the station ran a slanted but accurate story:

While some of what News 9's investigation found may seem like EBT abuse, the state is following the rules laid down by the state and federal governments that allow the cards to be used freely. Tracking each purchase is possible, but officials said the state runs the risk of becoming a sort of social police, and it could require more people and more money.

"If we get into the business of tracking why people are traveling 40 miles into Massachusetts, we're talking a relatively expensive infrastructure," Smith said. "That would require us to call each client and dig into their personal lives."

I've always been proud of New Hampshire, including the media. We have our issues, but we do very much try to get it right. Eventually.

The biggest part of the debate around EBT usage, though, wasn't about where people could use their benefits, but about *What is a life necessity?*

Soon after the store clerk in Peterborough refused to sell cigarettes to the EBT customer, I was called in front of the legislature to discuss the issue. Some on that legislative committee had hopes of casting blame on government —that is to say, me and the Department—for not doing more to ensure proper purchases were being made with EBT cards. The questioning of these few members ran along the same lines as the news reporter's had been: "What are you doing to ensure EBT is being used for life necessities?" My response was this:

I think everyone here agrees that using EBT for cigarettes and beer is inappropriate. The Department agrees that is true. But after that, it gets murky. For instance, many of our clients live in substandard unsafe neighborhoods. Should they be allowed to buy guns with their EBT cash benefits to protect themselves? Some in the legislature might say they have that right. Others might take an anti-gun approach. These are not decisions you want a government agency to make. They are far more appropriately left to you, the people's representatives.

The Associate Commissioner I worked for at the time was in the audience. She chastised me later for using the gun example. Not for the first time she left me scratching my head because it was exactly the kind of controversial example that would trigger the debate for a subset of legislators—not so much against each other—but against themselves as they wondered what the right answer should be. But that's what this book is about. Welfare in   America would be more satisfying for all stakeholders if we could just talk honestly about the truths of it, rather than being paralyzed by fartworms consumed by the career fear of controversy.

Various legislators offered solutions. One suggested that the appearance of the EBT card might be changed to prevent fraud. (See the image of New Hampshire's sample card below.) There already was a federal mandate that the client's name be embossed on the card, but it was useless. For one thing, any benefit of having the person's name on the card was cancelled out by a different federal requirement that all family members have access to the card to purchase food. A sick mom, for instance, may need to send her twelve-year-old to a pharmacy to pick up a prescription. What good does mom's name on the card do when her child is using it? Moreover, today's modern families may have members with different last names, so adding, say,

"Smith Family" to the card cannot be a universal solution, and the card is too small to add all family members individually. Another option was to put a photo on the card. That wasn't possible for the reasons just listed. Yet another option would be to issue an individual card to each family member in each cash case. But that would not only add new costs by doubling or tripling the number of card issuances, it would be of limited value since pre-teens and early teenaged children don't have identifications to check against the name anyway.

Photos on cards and names on cards make no sense. EBT technology piggybacks on credit card technology. You swipe the card, enter your PIN, and the transaction is complete. For a photograph to have value, the grocery store would have to identify every purchase as being EBT. Then it would have to stop the transaction, ask to see the card, then ask for an identification to look for a match. When someone in the legislature posed this as a possi-

bility, the New Hampshire Grocer's Association came out adamantly opposed. They not only did not want to be the EBT police, but they didn't want to hold up their checkout lanes doing it. Thus neither a name nor a photograph on the card carries any practical advantage, and requiring an ID of a recipient to match against the card thereby also carries no practical advantage.

Another legislator suggested that clients not be allowed to access cash, but make all payments electronically. I explained the issue with this was the number of life-essentials that do not accept electronic payment, including but not limited to: landlords, child care, Laundromats, town clerks (taxes; car registrations; parking tickets); bus transits, road tolls, school fees, and so on.

Another suggestion was to require cash recipients keep receipts and prove to my eligibility workers that purchases were for life essentials each month before getting their next cash benefit. Yeesh! Think about that one. Even little New Hampshire had over 14,000 cash recipients. Checking every receipt from every purchase by every client every month, when currently we touched the case only once every six months, would have meant adding six times the government workers to do the new work. And even then, who's to say the client didn't trash the receipt from their own "bad" purchase and fish someone else's "good" receipt out of the garbage to show us?

It was also suggested that the Department might "vendor" pay life-essentials that do not accept electronic transactions. That is to say, government would direct pay a welfare recipient's bills, like rent, heat, phone, and so on. Double Yeesh! I explained that to do that a living budget for every client would be necessary in order to establish the proper amount to vendor-pay to each billing agency. And every time a client changed addresses, it would have to be reported and new billing assignments created. Then what if the change was reported, but we didn't get it until after we'd already sent money to the old billing agent? Staffing requirements to meet the logistics of this suggestion were massive. Meanwhile, as we've already seen, the size of the monthly cash grant was less than the rent clients were being charged. Now what? Since there isn't enough money for all the bills, would government assume responsibility for limiting payments for any one life-essential at expense of another? That would leave the government open to liability for misfortunes resulting from such a choice. Say, for instance, we underfunded heating oil so as to pay rent money to the landlord, then the winter temperature outside drops to ten below zero leaving the welfare recipient freezing with no heat. It would have been interesting, though, if legislators had to get up front and personal with what life necessities actually cost a welfare recipient, compared to what they received in benefits.

Another legislator suggested limiting cash access at ATM's to $25. That followed zero logic since ATM's charge conservatively $2.50 for cash withdrawals. Even though EBT clients get a few free, that suggestion would have cost a client about $70 in ATM fees just to withdraw $750 to pay rent. And that would be when the cash grant was already less than their rent by $75.

The suggestion that confused legislators most was whether EBT technology could automatically block certain types of purchases. There is, unfortunately, a fundamental difference between cash and food stamps on the EBT card. First, for Food Stamps, USDA limits authorization to accept food stamps to specific retailers they've investigated as appropriate. As a condition of this authorization, the grocer installs a Point of Sale Device with a specific payment button called "EBT." This button must be pushed for food stamps to be used out of the EBT card. Now the checkout clerk can manually screen out items prohibited by food stamp policy, such as diapers or laundry detergent. Most retailers have adopted computer systems to automate approval of food stamp purchases.

None of this happens for EBT cash. When an EBT card is used to access cash benefits in the retailer's checkout lane, the Point of Sale device cannot distinguish it as EBT from any other bank debit card transaction. The EBT card is in effect invisible to the retailer. The logistical problems and costs associated with blocking, say, cigarette purchases from being purchased with an EBT card, are enormous.

In the end, these and other suggestions did appear as legislative proposals, but failed to gain support. In short order, the legislature came up with a couple of different bills to restrict what might be purchased with an EBT card. I note ironically that prohibiting guns was in one of them, not in the other. Fortunately the Health, Human Services and Elderly Affairs Committee in the New Hampshire House was made up of practical and responsible House Representatives, both Republican and Democrat.

I showed them that EBT could not automate restricting specific purchases, such as beer or cigarettes. As always, though, if that was the will of the people I'd be happy to develop something, as long as everyone knew it would be costly and would require additional fraud investigators and cooperation from retailers like Walmart who sold cigarettes, beer and such.

On the other hand, I also showed them a free solution. The EBT contractor had a new technology that could automate blocking EBT at certain *types* of retailers using the Merchant Category Code.

Ultimately that's what happened. By 2014, under federal law, EBT Cards had already been restricted at liquor stores, gaming establishments, and adult entertainment facilities that involved disrobing. Then in 2014 the New Hampshire legislature passed House Bill 219, which added new locations to the list of those restricted from accessing EBT cash. These new locations included: branding, body piercing, and tattoo shops; smoke shops; and recreational marijuana dispensaries.

And at last EBT was out of the news.

CHAPTER 11
Vampires Suck at Job Interviews

S ince the general civilization of mankind, I believe there are more instances of the abridgment of the freedom of the people, by gradual and silent encroachments of those in power, than by violent and sudden usurpations. --James Madison

Okay. We've established that welfare in America is flawed. It neither serves as a safe place for children, nor does it work to systemically move American children out of poverty through employment of parents. But the laws are in place to make these things happen, so what stands in the way of just fixing all that?

Leadership.

Americans often expect government to be run like a business. They assume leaders who run welfare programs will be doing the people's business, accomplishing what is set out in law for them. Most Americans trust welfare leaders—well, in a watchful way—to be knowledgeable and focused on their jobs because that's our experience with how the free enterprise world works.

Is that trust naïve?

Yes, for two reasons.

First, Government cannot be run like a business. Second, the process for selecting welfare leaders is slipshod. In fact, it's as if the whole system was invented to be dysfunctional. It starts like this.

As we've said, welfare in colonial America was administered mainly by volunteers in churches, charities, and towns who were unpaid or paid very little. The job was mostly an expression of personal values. What changed?

The Social Security Act in 1935.

The Social Security Act involved the federal government in welfare for the first time. Since then State welfare agencies have become the apex hog waffling in the trough of the State's starvation budget. That's because welfare agencies oversee a broad array of costly programs like Medicaid, public health, child protection, child support, child care, mental health, drug abuse, food stamps, cash welfare, EBT, services for seniors, some veterans affairs, and more. And to run these programs welfare agencies require a small army of civil servants. They need workers who do eligibility, followed by quality control workers who monitor the eligibility workers, and managers and supervisors for all of them, followed by support staff, finance staff, human resources staff....

Cash and food assistance—which have been this book's focus—are usually only a portion of the welfare run by such agencies.

But you knew all that already.

The point is that State human service agencies have become so big they are super-magnets for ambitious egos because leadership of these agencies offers elite political power, constant media opportunities, maximum prestige, and a high public profile. A job as Commissioner of such an agency is a solid stepping stone to the Governor's office, to a judgeship, or maybe to the US House of Representatives. So what type of person is likely to be drawn to the job—or more importantly, likely to get *selected* for the job—of having apex control over the well-being of a State's disadvantaged children, seniors, and persons with disabilities?

Only the most caring, responsible, and business savvy people, right?

Right?

Let's start by recalling that for any government to make progress in any way, the stars must align.

First, State agencies are in the Executive Branch. That means a State's Governor will almost invariably nominate a Commissioner candidate from among his or her trusted political allies. That's the first cut. But if you'd expect it to be a slam dunk that the Governor would logically nominate an ally who has some slight connection with the Department they're going to lead, you'd be wrong. In fact, as they say in basketball when a player flubs a slam dunk, you "blew the bunny."

Here's a bunny for you. On February 15, 2017, New Hampshire's television station WMUR reported, "A businessman who homeschooled his children and has no professional background in public education is officially New Hampshire's next education Commissioner." (This example is not welfare, but close enough.) In essence what happened was, not only did the Governor nominate a new Commissioner who had zero experience as an educator, the candidate had zero experience even as a parent of a child who went to a public school. Now he's the Commissioner of the Department of Education.

That is one big head-scratcher. That is, until we review the political history.

Turns out the new Education Commissioner was the Governor's biggest challenger in the Primary. The Commissioner lost the Primary to the Governor by just 7/10ths of a percentage point. However, instead of demanding a recount as he might have, the soon-to-be candidate for Commissioner appeared at a press conference throwing his support entirely to the now Governor for the general election. So later, when the Governor nominated his new ally to be Commissioner, he was likely keeping his end of a tacit political bargain. The new Education Commissioner was confirmed—along party lines—as Education Commissioner not because he knew anything about education, but as an act of patronage.

Lesson one about a welfare Commissioner's selection. It's not necessary to have experience or investment in the mission of the job to be nominated. Those qualities are not among the stars that must align.

What political spin could possible sell the viability of this new Education Commissioner anyway? Well, as WMUR also reported, his backers said his "business background" would be an asset.

So let's go there for a moment. This business of "Leaders should run government like a business" is such a commonly held assumption we really should look at it. It is, in fact, one of the most commonly abused myths guiding the selection of government leaders.

Okay, I agree it makes a sort of visceral sense that being versed in the discipline of free enterprise business should translate well into bringing discipline to an inefficient, disorganized, self-serving government, or that improvements in government could easily happen if only flunky bureaucrats would get out of the way and stop blocking progress. That about sum it up? Well, it does make some seductive sense.

But here's the thing. Our example above—the education Commissioner who was ignorant about education—shows us a primary reason why government and business cannot be even close to the same. Commissioners are given a four year contract that not even a new Governor can break without cause. I ask you, would the Board of a big diaper corporation ever hire a new CEO who doesn't know their diapers, who has never pinned/taped a diaper on their own squalling infant, or who doesn't have at least genuine experience with manufacturing and marketing of infant goods? Only in government—not business—are leadership decisions made for the kind of bald, unapologetic, political, fartworm reasons that brought selection of an Education Commissioner who had no education about education…in short who was utterly unqualified to hold the job.

TERRY SMITH

Government can't be like Business because Business makes decisions based on cold logic. In the free market, the target is big, bold, and zeroed in: *profit*. Even when it's a for-profit company that is values-based, profit either rules or no more company. Corporate politics will of course play a role in promotion of staff to CEO[20], but hiring mistakes are more or less quickly corrected based on profit performance. Unlike the Commissioner of a state government agency, the CEO of a business doesn't often, if ever, get an ironclad mandatory four year term to be CEO regardless how badly that person does their job.

The differences between business and government go much, much deeper, though. Government is conducted under the microscopic scrutiny of a gaggle of squabblers: the state's legislature. Government cannot make "business" decisions without corresponding law permitting them to act, a process that particularly plays out during the biennial budget process.

The budget process. In New Hampshire, state agencies must develop a budget every other year. Around November the state agency finishes their proposed budget in secret and sends it to the Governor, who reviews it top to bottom in secret discussions with agency heads and makes whatever revisions. Once done, the Governor releases his budget with speeches and fanfare to the public in January. Welfare initiatives, benefit levels, staffing sizes…all of it is in the budget. And already the Commissioner of the welfare Department is one step removed from being in control of their "business" as now the purse strings controlling the business are the Governor's hands. But okay. It's a bit like having a corporation's Board approval.

Next the Governor's budget goes to the House Finance Committee for the House of Representatives to get a crack at it, making the Commissioner now two steps removed from his business. Things get particularly interesting if the House is controlled by a different political party than the Governor because then the fight over purse strings can actually be an intense political fight over social and fiscal policy with the Commissioner caught in the middle. During this phase the House Finance Committee reviews each budget item, sometimes line by line, while a representative from the welfare agency sits before them ready to answer questions. In my experience, they usually asked lucid and penetrating questions with an eye to controlling taxpayer spending—which is what taxpayers legitimately expect of them and which has the effect of defining priorities. But they also make social policy by opting to fund or not fund specific programs.

Let's ratchet this up yet another notch. Who does the welfare agency's leader choose to answer welfare questions in front of House Finance? Clearly

---

[20] For a fascinating read on how politics play out in organizations, see Henry Mintzberg, *Mintzberg on Management* (New York: The Free Press, 1989), 236-241.

the agency has subject matter experts who can advise the Governor's budget team, then later House Finance, about the need for certain welfare spending options, right. But are these subject matter experts brought in?

Maybe.

Every new Commissioner begins their four year term with what I call the "Six Month Mind Muddle." That is, during the first six months, every new Commissioner faces the reality of the job. Conservative leaders who are appointed, for instance, almost always learn to respect the challenges facing the Department as it goes about its missions. Liberal leaders, on the other hand, learn how the democratic process limits their initiatives. One thing is unwavering among all of them. Nearly every new Commissioner comes in convinced they can do a better job than the Commissioner before them. But to do that, they need to surround themselves with the best and brightest, right? Good leaders surround themselves with really smart people?

During that initial six-month grace period, every Commissioner is casting about among career civil servants in the agency to determine who their inner circle will be. Who they choose is critical because these are the people the Commissioner will listen to for the next four years. Everything they hear will be filtered by this inner team. And for the most ambitious careerists in the agency this is crunch time as they begin a sycophantic rush to impress the new guy (in a non -gender sense). The new Commissioner, in turn, will be regarding them closely looking for four things. One, did his minions of choice help him get his job. Two, is the minion a blank slate, willing to agree enthusiastically with any priority the new Commissioner might have. Three, does the minion appear to be completely and unquestionably loyal to the new guy, starting with ready willingness to jettison any ideas and loyalties held over from the previous Commissioner. And four, the successful convert to the newly minted inner circle must be an extrovert because the promotion game here is about getting noticed and it's extroverts who get noticed.

Let's take a look at this last one. What's the problem with an inner circle of extroverts? What's the difference between, say, extroverts and introverts?

Extroverts get energy from social settings. Introverts prefer being alone. Extroverts talk … a lot. Introverts listen more. Extroverts are easily distracted, whereas introverts stay focused for long periods of time. Extroverts make decisions quickly, while introverts prefer to deliberate about an issue before deciding. Extroverts are exciting to be with. Introverts are considerably less visible. And that's why extroverts get into the inner circle, and introverts are most often overlooked, both according to their nature.[21]

---

[21] By the way, Thomas Jefferson was an introvert who lived quietly and delivered only two speeches during his Presidencies…the inaugural addresses.

But tell me. Who would you rather have making decisions? Think about it. A "decision" is a choice between various options, each option bringing with it a host of variables that must be weighed and compared. For instances, to buy shoes do you prefer the variable of comfort over the variable of style or the variable of cost or the variable of quality construction? By how much, a factor of 7 over 6 over 5 over 8?) Do you really want someone making decisions affecting the lives of people in poverty who doesn't take the time to identify all the variables, let alone examine them with focused reflection?

Extroverts can tend to make rash decisions, or what can be worse, *no* decisions.

One example I'll point to was a highly extroverted Associate Commissioner who continuously brought her division directors together in a room to brainstorm. Problem was, we brainstormed the same thing over and over again across a span of years because as a supreme extrovert she jolted with energy from the meeting itself. The real work—the hard-slogging, slow, detailed, in-your-face, boots-on-the-ground development of a project—required the strengths of not an extrovert, but an introvert. Inevitably the topic of these meetings never progressed beyond repetitive meetings and the time of talented staffers was wasted.

In the end, extroverts by nature get noticed, introverts don't (unless they generate some unusual accomplishment). New Commissioners either don't particularly take the time or interest to go slogging through Department history to uncover the best talent with the most accomplishments. After all, they look for people who remind them of themselves, since they're usually extroverts who themselves were chosen for their job by being visible. And too, introverts cannot be trusted. Reflective people may question decisions, may be uncooperative at times. Unwavering loyalty and personal support can be much more attractive to a new Commissioner trying to consolidate their power over an organization.

Too often the Commissioner chooses an inner-team based on obvious qualities rather than thoughtful ones. But at least people are always chosen from the ranks of civil servants who know the business, right?

That would be no.

Here's another example. One Commissioner I served under promoted a nurse from Public Health to lead the divisions that were responsible for welfare, child protection, elderly and adult services, homeless services, and juvenile justice. Why? Because allegedly the nurse had supported the Commissioner in his bid for the job and so a bit of *quid pro quo* was in order. Trust and loyalty had been proven. It was irrelevant that as a nurse she had no absolutely no clue about any of the program areas she was selected to oversee, nor had even been trained in administration. Yet it became her job to represent these program areas to the Commissioner and his inner circle at senior executive meetings. And it was she who was chosen to testify about welfare during the budget process to the Governor and the House Finance Committee.

So much for running government like a business. But we're not done.

No, not nearly.

After the House Finance is done with the budget they put it into two bills. One bill is the dollar spending plan itself, and the other bill aligns law with policy changes proposed in the budget.

Next, these two bills go to the Senate Finance Committee. And now the agency's CEO is three steps (Governor, House, Senate) removed from the budget for the agency's welfare "business." In the Senate phase of the budget, fiscal and social priorities almost always shift yet again. When the Senate is controlled by a different party than the Governor or the House or both, battle lines can get fiery. But even when the House and Senate are controlled by the same party, the Senate frequently disagrees with the House, so the two bodies go to a Committee of Conference to make necessary compromises. When they're done, the final result goes back to the Governor who may or may not sign it into law.

Welfare as a "business" is a bit more complicated for yet another reason. While the Department's budget is secret until the Governor is done with it, all budget sessions in both the House and the Senate Finance Committees are open to the public. *And the media.* Plenty of policies being considered are of general public concern, so the developing budget item can wind up being sensationalized in the news. After the news cycle breaks, while still in negotiations, legislators in both the Senate and the House Finance Committees are likely to hear from donors, constituents, and various political think tanks including out-of-state ones pushing their agenda one state at a time.

So run government like a business? Unlike business, in government the newspaper and television media are watching every detail of every decision. Decision-makers are apt to have widely varying opinions about policy that end up being compromises looking nothing like what the welfare agency—that is, the "business"—needs. Then add to the mix that agency experts aren't always brought in to testify to decision- makers, causing the legislature's understanding of policy to be incomplete. And then add in that Commissioner's and Associate Commissioners can be chosen in the first place who have no understanding of what their mission is, let alone have a vision for leading that mission, or even having the values of the mission in the first place.

The welfare system is one big ball of garbled string and the alley cats are having at it.

Let's for a moment look at it another way. Let's focus on how leaders are *not* selected. First, there is no competitive process wherein the best Commissioner candidates are brought in for interview by a team of subject matter experts, legislators, the Governor's office, and local stakeholders such as community service providers, advocates, think-tanks, and clients in the system. In short, all the stakeholders a Commissioner must please in the job are entirely absent from a public selection process for a new Commissioner.

The nomination and confirmation process does not systemically ensure that personal character, mission values, experience, accomplishments, or education are core considerations in hiring a competent Commissioner. Rather instead, political expediency and cronyism rules the process.

And that's where it gets scary.

The point of all this is only to make it clear that the commitment to the mission of welfare is not principal to the selection process for leadership in welfare, whereas politics and personal interests are very much endemic to the process. No systemic process ensures that the next welfare agency leader will be one who has either the skills or the administrative tools to effectively progress welfare in a way that brings recipients to employment, health and safety, while still being efficient with taxpayer dollars.

We're leaving the doors to the welfare blood bank unlocked. A poster is taped to the glass that drips viscous red paint inviting Dracula's children to browse through ... well, as long as they have the right party affiliation.

Your experience may vary, of course.

CHAPTER 12

In Music, Silence Is a Note

Since the selection of welfare commissioners is cavalier, the best we can hope for is that the agency sports strong civil service employees who have subject matter expertise. Next, we hope those civil servants are listened to.

But are they?

Fartworm decisions in welfare have real life consequences. In business, leaders are accountable to that, but in government, Commissioners have a four year appointment that takes a major infraction on their part to break. This arrangement has two major implications. First, commissioners can come in with little knowledge about welfare. And second, there's simply not enough time in a four year term to create a five year strategic plan. So mostly commissioners simply try to keep the welfare wheels turning, maybe tackling one or two specific issues of interest.

After all, isn't it progress if it isn't regression?

To begin to fully understand the implications, let start by determining exactly what welfare Commissioners *do* against what they're *supposed* to do. Here's one of the present mission statements from New Hampshire's Department of Health and Human Services:

To meet the basic human needs of New Hampshire citizens: The Department has a responsibility to provide financial, medical and emergency assistance and employment support services to those in need, in order to assist individuals in reaching self-sufficiency. (NH Department of Health and Human Services website)

Okay. In terms of welfare and establishing what a Commissioner is responsible for, this mission statement sets a stage. It morosely lacks any expectation that the services provided be of *quality*, but as far as it goes, okay.

What, then, does State law say about welfare? Is that any better in terms of establishing quality? In New Hampshire RSA 167:7 "Amount of Assistance" does set some qualifiers:

167:7 Amount of Assistance.

II. *The commissioner of health and human services shall establish for the aid to families with dependent children* [now called Temporary Assistance to Needy Families, or *TANF] consolidated standards of need, or consolidated standards of need except for shelter, which may be separate from the payment standards and which shall be annually revised to accurately reflect the current cost of the basic necessities of living compatible with decency and health as determined by reliable market data. The commissioner may further establish consolidated standards of payment, or consolidated standards of payment except for shelter, subject to appropriated funds and applicable federal regulations.*

III. **The commissioner of health and human services shall determine the level of benefits** *in both programs so that recipients shall be allowed to subsist compatibly with decency and health, subject to the amount of appropriated funds and applicable federal regulations.*

Now this gets a bit tricky. Note that 167:7(II) gives the Commissioner power to do two things. One, establish a "standard of need" and two, establish a standard of payment. The standard of need is a dollar amount that welfare clients need in order to live in "decency and health as determined by reliable market data." But does this mean that the Commissioner adjusts the size of welfare cash assistance to single mothers each year to reflect inflation or market data?

That would be "no."

Why? Because notably the law states that in addition to the "standard of need," the Commissioner must develop a separate "standard of payment," which is the amount that is actually provided to recipients. Each year the division I directed, the Division of Family Assistance, determined an updated "standard of need" using market surveys as we're supposed to, so we always knew how much money a single mother needed for basic necessities each month to keep the child in "decency and health." And each year we published the survey finding. And each year it was ignored and the actual payment size never changed.

What does the imbalance look like? As of October 1, 2017—that is, even the month *after* we increased the TANF grant to 60% of federal poverty—the "standard of need" to live in decency and health in New Hampshire was $4,002 for a mom with two children. Yet the amount of actual assistance was $1,021.

How exactly did that play out?

This way. Good commissioners assign subject matter experts to testify to the Governor and legislature on budget and program issues who are steeped in deep knowledge and long experience about welfare. But poor commissioners are jealous of the limelight or they're afraid an underling will say something in testimony that will be a surprise or embarrassment to them. So instead they send someone from their inner circle, say an Associate Commissioner, to testify about programs and policies. Unfortunately the Associate Commissioner typically has nowhere near the expertise needed to properly advise decision makers and can wind up fumbling badly with severe consequences. In the end, funding for needed policy changes may never see the light of day because the right people are not there to present the argument. As a glaring example, for several budgets prior to 2017, commissioners in New Hampshire sent ill-informed members of their inner circle to testify to the Governor and legislative finance committees on the welfare budget. The real life consequence was that TANF cash assistance remained inadequate because no one could explain it to them clearly. There's no guarantee that the Governor or legislature would have listened anyway, but the case was not plainly made and TANF children suffered unnecessary housing evictions and other poverty-related hardship as a result.

So, back to the question. What is a Commissioner *supposed* to do, and what *do* they do?

Each Commissioner is different. They come to the job with different levels of experience, energy and commitment. Here are a few examples of how commissioners treat their job and welfare.

One Commissioner I served under was appointed to the job running New Hampshire's human services agency for four years, but served just nine months. Why? He committed an infraction.

As the Concord Monitor reported on September 11, 2003, "New Health and Human Services Commissioner...has resigned amid criticism that he was serving as co-chairman of a national political action committee." The news article continued, "[The Commissioner also] came under attack late last week for seeking investors for a private insurance company he wanted to start." Meanwhile, all this came to light amid questions about how he managed to serve as Commissioner while also coaching a high school football team. Sadly what this Commissioner is most remembered for—other than that scandal—is that the toilet in his office on the fourth floor overflowed once, soaked through the floor, and leaked executive sewer onto the 3rd floor desk of an accountant in the Finance division.

Perhaps the moral of the story is, *You can't run a Department by the seat of your pants when they're wrapped around your ankles.*

Life, though, is never black-and-white. To be fair, by all accounts this Commissioner was a good man heavily involved in State charity work. And he cared about kids enough to devote his time coaching high school sports. That may actually make him one of the better adjusted Commissioners. But it also makes him an example of a commissioner who was not only unqualified, but conflicted about the mission.

Here's an example of another commissioner. What was he *supposed* to do, and what *did* he do?

What he was *supposed* to do.

It seems odd to suggest, but the biggest innovation needed desperately in welfare today is creation of a list of all the agency's programs and services. A department inventory of programs and services has always seemed a no-brainer to me. Can you imagine a supermarket manager who does not inventory shelves regularly to ensure the store is properly stocked? Doesn't it make sense to know what products fly off the shelves and what products take up room and expense but never sell? Smart supermarkets have long ago automated that inventory process, linking scanned items at the checkout lane to the central computer database.

That's how the State welfare agency could be run like a business.

For State government welfare, an inventory of services should not be an innovation, but apparently it is. Civil service subject matter experts in New Hampshire's welfare agency have pressed for this for over twenty years. In 2007, I chaired a team of civil service leaders from all over the Department to look at how we served children. This was an extra meeting for everyone, but the people who came were mission-driven civil service. We called the team the Child Well-Being Task Force. Here's the system transformation we recommended:

When someone comes to the agency looking for any kind of help for a child, they should get a) an assessment to determine what issues they have that need help; and b) directly connected to the services they need through a soft-handoff, not just some referral to call a number.

How radical is that? In the end, apparently pretty much so.

See, the way most human services agencies work in reality is, clients come to the system asking for a particular program—say, food stamps—having identified it themselves. They have to because State welfare agencies assume that clients know what among the agency's various programs and services to ask for.

They don't.

How could they when the agency itself has itself never done its own inventory of services? That means even workers in the agency don't know what programs and services are available. A client, then, may have figured out they need food stamps, but they may not be aware they can receive WIC, or that the Child Support Division can help them track down that missing parent, or that the agency can help them get a job and find child care, or that the agency can help them out of a domestic violence situation.

Think of the child who comes in with mom to apply for food stamps. The child's baby teeth are rotted little black stumps, usually caused because they were put to bed with the bottle of milk still in their mouth. The worker doing eligibility may happen to see those missing teeth, but do they do anything? Maybe. The worker may have been around long enough to know there's a person at State Office who may in turn know if there's a dental program for low income children, and then the worker may go the extra mile to make a phone call to that central office person, and then that central office person may actually pick up the phone.... This is decidedly not a systemic process.

Another example is this. The opioid crisis hit New Hampshire hard, causing many addicted parents to lose their children. Most grandparents in New Hampshire did not know that when they took custody of their grandchild, they could apply for TANF. Those few that did know, *didn't* know they could apply for *just* the grandchild, meaning we wouldn't count the grandparents' income against the child's eligibility.[22] Grandparents were being denied assistance because they thought they had to apply for cash assistance for themselves along with their grandchildren, in which case we did count their income and they were almost always not eligible.

What *did* the commissioner do?

Did our State welfare agency explain things to these grandparents? No. On the contrary. The Commissioner's inner circle instead instituted a quota of some sixty phone calls a day for each welfare eligibility worker, and now the worker's performance evaluation is based not on how well they served the need, but on how little time they spent with clients. The basic contradiction here is that eligibility workers are on the phone with people desperately trying to navigate a potpourri of services they don't understand, so they can put food on the table for their children or pay their rent before they're evicted. But because now workers' chance for promotion and salary increases are at risk, desperate people are treated to swift conclusions before

---

[22] Wait, this is good policy: it's not only cheaper for the State than paying for foster care, but it's also better for the child to stay with family when possible. And, of course, there aren't enough foster care parents in the first place.

the full conversation is completed. This quota system raised such a problem that one of our local town welfare administrators phoned me to complain. (Town welfare administrators provide supplemental assistance to low income people to what we in the State provide.) She had contacted the state welfare agency to ask whether three of her local welfare clients were receiving State assistance yet.

The eligibility worker told her to phone back separately for each one of her clients. That is, phone back three times.

What?

See, systemically, to meet their daily quota, the worker needed to get credit for three phone calls instead of one.

In the end, the State welfare agency's application system was constructed to be rushed, which is of course just exactly the opposite of what is necessary if the intent is truly to build a client-oriented intake assessment.[23] Civil service veterans warned against this system and gave the Commissioner options for providing call center efficiencies in a way that was more compatible with human services, but the agency's Commissioner came from a free enterprise technology company. He wanted the win of bringing technological progress to government despite that it contradicted the agency's mission.

But wait. It gets perverted.

Let's return to the Child Well-Being Task Force for a moment, where we recommended to the commissioner that the Department a) build a front end client assessment tool, b) conduct an inventory of agency programs and services, and c) build a database to keep all these services straight and updated. The database should be searchable by both our own workers *and* the public and it should allow clients to be tracked so every worker helping that person would know what other programs the client is involved in. That way we could treat the client as a whole. Pay particular attention to the word "whole."

In 2007, the Child Well-Being Task Force invited the Commissioner in to hear our recommendations and asked for his buy-in. He walked away pledging his support, but we never saw him again and eventually we disbanded, unable to get resources to move forward.

Then it gets perverted. The Commissioner later picked up on the theme. He established a new committee to look at No Wrong Door, a way for clients to enter the agency and be treated for all their needs. The new committee brainstormed the issue all over again and not surprisingly came up with the

---

[23] No analysis was ever done to determine the cost of clients calling back later for additional programs, or because their initial contact had left them confused. Nor has the agency examined increased monetary costs to the State, or human costs to the safety of children, for not listening to client needs sooner. The agency's intake system was built because the Commissioner thought it was a good idea, not because anyone had looked at empiric data to determine whether it in truth was a good idea.

same thing the Child Well Being Task Force had already recommended. But while the Commissioner created the committee, it was either just for show or he didn't know how to operationalize the findings. In any case, he dedicated no resources to implement change.

Later, after the No Wrong Door committee was abandoned, he started a new project else called Service Integration. Same idea as No Wrong Door, same withholding of resources, same abandonment. Later he yet again started up the idea, this time under the new name of Integrated Service Delivery. Same idea as No Wrong Door, same withholding of resources, same abandonment.

And finally the ultimate perversion.

The commissioner invented a catch phrase: "Whole Person." The idea was the same as No Wrong Door and all the others: that is, the Department needed not just to look at what the client was applying for, but to serve the client's full range of needs. He used this catch phrase ubiquitously for the rest of his term as the agency's welfare leader. In a fascinating manipulation of reality, he built the impression that he actually had a plan, whereas in reality this was a formidable example of what's called "the big lie," which we'll talk about momentarily, because instead of acting with commitment to build an assessment tool, or to do an inventory of programs, or to create a database to help serve the full needs of people, he acted just the opposite by putting limits on how long workers could talk to clients. His telephone call quota system interfered with the front end communication process instead of allowing for investigation of the whole person's needs. Insofar as inventorying Department services, he declared in a meeting that "We tried that. It's too complicated." (Too complicated?) And instead of building a database for the "whole person," he built one to determine where agency money was being spent in the state, a database that never demonstrated much utility. In the end, it was just so much black smoke billowing from the smokestack of a diesel fartworm idling in the parking lot. Yet because he used the term "whole person" as if he truly meant it, he was credited with progress he never even attempted.

But look. The commissioner mentioned above was at heart a good man, well-intentioned. Despite strong personal values, his tragic flaw was that he insulated himself on the top floor of the building with his inner circle. I suspect he even believed his rhetoric about the whole person, just he would have known better if he had only listened to his experienced civil service staff. In any case, the purpose of this book is not to give a shellacking to any particular commissioner. What's at stake here is much bigger. What's at stake is that leadership in the welfare system generally is wormy and you in the public deserve to see why it fails you.

So do commissioners *do* what they're *supposed* to do?

Some do, but others don't. Of the ones who don't, how do they get away with it? One way is to distract the organization. The most common strategy for distracting that commissioners often resort to is the "reorganization" ploy. By moving units in the organization around—like boxes—the commissioner cements their authority, looks like a leader, and keeps civil service staff stressed about where they might wind up working next and, worse, whether they'll even have a job in the end. Staff tends not to criticize the executioner when their neck is already on the chopping block and the axe is indecisively poised.

But the most outlandish strategy to distract the world about inept leadership…is "the big lie."

CHAPTER 13

First Rule of The Power Elite: Never Talk Smack About Another Leader

*T*he size of the lie is a definite factor in causing it to be believed, for the vast masses of the nation are in the depths of their hearts more easily deceived than they are consciously and intentionally bad. The primitive simplicity of their minds renders them a more easy prey to a big lie than a small one, for they themselves often tell little lies but would be ashamed to tell a big one. -- Adolph Hitler, *Mein Kampf*

When leaders of any organization—welfare or not—provide staff with information, people instinctively want to hear it as the truth. When commissioners make a decision, their staff are predisposed to view it as good. We cannot conclude a conversation about welfare leadership without a discussion as to why.

The discussion begins with two observations. One is *The Big Lie*. The second is *System Justification*.

These are the duo of ungodly ghouls, the haunting wraiths that swirl through the choking ether of our worst nightmares. They're the undead fingers that rise up through the crumbled dirt of ancient graves to clutch at our ankles and drag us back down into the rotted soil of musty tombs where hopes go to die. If mankind is doomed to extinction because of anything in the deepest, blackest part of our common human psyche, it is these two human traits.

The Big Lie.

When the Commissioner broadcast the message of "the whole person," he did not follow up with any remotely credible substance. When the leader from the USDA Food and Nutrition Service testified to Congress that the food stamp error rate was continually improving, they were accepted as truthful despite there actually being a conspiracy of secrecy. Whether intentionally conceived or just a mad fantasy, when leaders lie, they remain unquestioned. Well, at least until a lie reaches critical mass.

Why is that?

Some theorists think that the human trust mechanism is innate to our evolution beginning when our early ancestors loped on their knuckles in small bands the size of baboon troops. We eventually grew bigger and smarter brains, but even so, we continued to live in small hunter/gatherer clusters. The theory of "the Big Lie" is that in such small communities no person—especially a leader—could get away with lying. Too many people knew the leader intimately. After all, everyone slept on the ground within snoring distance. There was no hiding. Humans evolved with a trusting nature because they could believe what they could see and they could see everything. If the band's leader said something hard-to-believe, why then it had to be that the leader knew stuff you didn't, and probably that was the case.

But there's more.

Theorists also postulate that being in small bands, we evolved to trust each other because we were competing for food and territory against "strangers" in other bands. In other words, trust each other, but not the other guy from that other band because they were probably trying to encroach on your territory, steal your food, accost your mate. The theory makes sense. In primitive societies, nothing less than survival is dependent on trust for one other against the outsider, the common enemy. It's the same factor reported by soldiers that the heat of battle isn't about lofty ideals like patriotism as much as it is covering the backs of buddies in the field.

So when a Commissioner is on our team and tells us we're building a system for the whole person, our instinct is to believe him despite total lack of evidence to support. It takes a major infraction to unseat that innate trust in leaders.

I don't know if these theories are accurate, though they do have some ring of truth to them. What I do know is that at a minimum rank and file people in America—not just civil servants—have their own problems in their own day-to-day lives. They are neither omniscient nor omnipotent. They have no choice but to trust in leaders to take care of the big stuff so they don't have to, and they're only too happy to hear that things are going well, or believe the lies if they're not, so they can get back to what they were doing, at least until a leader's lies reach critical mass.

So there is a big lie in welfare and systemically it is this. Not only do we not hire Commissioners and other leaders based on knowledge and qualifications and interest in the mission over self-interest. No. We additionally don't even necessarily hire people who are intrinsically good persons. How can we reconcile the contradiction of a welfare system that does not systemically bring in leaders interested in the welfare of people both inside and outside the welfare agency? How is it we can be so wrong in our expectations?

System Justification.

There's another theory that might help answer that question. It is a phenomenon called "system justification." Also variously known as "cognitive biases," "group think," or "false consciousness," along with some elements of the deeply subconscious human yearning for a "benevolent dictator." These are all pretty much permutations of the same thing. Namely, Modern Man has evolved predisposed to view their existence in a positive way.

According to this theory, we humans have a psychological need to feel good about ourselves and the world around us. As a result, we defend ourselves with a variety of defense mechanisms like denial and projection and so on, and defend our social order by accepting its prevailing tenets. We may, for instance, attribute truth to the myth that people with low social status—such as welfare recipients—are innately unworthy, maybe even out of touch with god. In this way, when the world around us feels in conflict or turmoil—as it inevitably will at times—we can remain locked into our "normal" to avoid stress and confusion, regardless of the evidence around us to the contrary.

What is particularly weird about this phenomenon is that it applies to people in the lower social orders also. For example, we all know that people of privilege indulge in cronyism and patronage to reward themselves in the power elite class. Rich people, after all, keep getting richer, while the poor not so much. Yet perversely, the *un*-privileged people among us often support that very patronage among the elite even when it acts against their own self-interests. They may, for example, support tax cuts for the wealthy that will ultimately cost themselves in the impoverished class more. According to systems justification theory, the motivation is that by linking themselves in support of the elite, un-privileged people are identifying themselves as part of the winning team (the rich), not as a member of the lower social order to which they really belong. According to this theory, we all of us are drawn to defending the status quo—even when we are not being rewarded by it—because deviation from the "normal" brings feelings of loss, risk, and stress. So instead we rationalize ways to fool ourselves into thinking everything is just fine as they are, even when we are reminded frequently that things are *not* just fine.

In the end, the odds are stacked against meaningful change in welfare. Experienced civil servants may see need for systemic change, but must navigate an array of impediments to persuade the agency's inner circle into making that change. It's unfortunate, but that's just the way government works, so get over it. Right?

Right?

Well what if it leads to murder?

The people served by a human services agency live life on the edge. Their very lives are more at risk than middle class America, and certainly more so than the elites that comprise welfare leadership. And that's the point of this whole discussion about leadership in welfare. When leaders in human services botch things, very, very bad things can happen.

Let's return to the example of the nurse. When a new commissioner was campaigning for the job, he allegedly received help from a friend, a nurse who was running the welfare agency's Division of Public Health. The commissioner got the job and rewarded the nurse by making her the associate commissioner in charge of welfare, including child protection.

Let's reiterate. This commissioner put someone in charge of the safety of children who had neither education nor experience with child protection.

What happened?

Two toddlers were murdered in a few years span who had been in the welfare agency's system under the watch of this administrator.[24] Child protection didn't save them because this nurse had not the skills to see and adjust to organizational warning signs in the child protection system she'd been given to oversee. What's more, she's still out there. When a newer commissioner came aboard, the nurse had lost her power base in the Department and so left New Hampshire to take a job out-of-state...*before* she was held accountable. The director of that division also retired before the deaths were publicly linked to the State. But to satisfy the community, the Governor fired yet a third person, a hapless civil servant who was not a primary leader when the fractured system was being built. No one has ever held the commissioner accountable who was in charge of it all at the time. But then again, to be fair, think about it. The commissioner was in charge of the agency, but the Governors and legislatures he worked with made the final decisions. This was government, not "business."

The general public in New Hampshire was outraged about the deaths of babies, under State supervision, as ought we all be. To their credit the legislature stepped in to create several oversight committees to review the child protection system. In a way, this is a progressive outcome, because child protection has now been removed a small distance from the fartworm welfare leadership selection process. But the whole mess was tainted from the start because one commissioner looked at the wrong things when

---

[24] http://www.concordmonitor.com/New-Hampshire-Commission-to-make-DCYF-oversight-director-recommendations-private-13737445

choosing his inner circle. And one fartworm nurse allowed her ambition to outstrip her abilities.

Leadership selection in welfare is dysfunctional. It was literally fatal to someone already living on the edge. That is not acceptable.

Government does have one protection against bad leaders. The civil service. To ensure consistency of subject matter expertise, civil service employees are notoriously difficult to fire. That, of course, sometimes griped me when I had poor performers who I couldn't get rid of. Ultimately, though, the protection is for good reasons. Without civil service protections, a new commissioner could fire the State's expert on, say, Temporary Assistance to Needy Families, then hire someone new. Then four years later the next commissioner could fire *that* person. Government would be an endless cycle of people purge and burn. No one would last long enough in the job to become an expert.

Under that scenario, everyone—the people using the program, the people administering the program, the legislature, the taxpayer—everyone would be confused because no one would be left to lead on program policy. Everyone would lose as the business of welfare would become a power grab to generate an organization loyal to one thing: the commissioner, not the mission of welfare. Civil service protections ensure that commissioners come and go, but career experts stay to advise every next commissioner. The commissioner doesn't always *listen* to their experts, of course. Even when they do, they don't always understand the policy nuances. But the opportunity for success is there. And some commissioners, the ones who do actually listen, like the one who helped guide TANF work reforms in 2006, can be highly successful.

Yet even civil service employees are not safe from fartworms. One commissioner in New Hampshire, for instance, came into power and within twenty-four months had fired or driven out nineteen veteran leaders in the Department. It happened surreptitiously over a period of time, until just suddenly one afternoon I went to a meeting with about ten other director level people, looked around the room, and realized I only recognized one other person. Friends and colleagues I'd built trust with over my twenty-six years were just suddenly missing, many without a word of goodbye, just here one day, gone the next.

You can measure the essence of leadership by the quality of people fleeing it.

I reached out to a few from among the exodus. One had been the leader of the Department's Human Resources, who had watched the beginning of this personnel purging first hand. He confided that the stress had gotten to be too much because the commissioner had constantly engaged in unethical personnel actions. Another high ranking worker said she was leaving before the commissioner could put the blame on her for something as he had others. A third with nearly thirty years of experience shook his head saying, "This is the most political animal I've seen as commissioner." Some leaders in the Department just disappeared overnight with no jobs waiting for them. Evidence seems to indicate a bald pattern of premeditated staff isolation and excision.

It's a manifestation of the Big Lie that exists like a squirming earwig burrowing wetly through the human brain. Especially when said by a person in power, the commissioner's accusation against a staff member assumes the aura of fact. When it happens, the rest of the herd in the organization watches nervously as one of their own goes down, throat clamped firmly in the jaws of the chief executive, already forgetting as they turn back to their daily grazing, or perhaps falling victim to a related paradigm called *Schadenfreude*, which is the human tendency to find glee in the misfortune of others. At this writing, men across the country are being accused by women of sexual harassment and assault. We all agree this is long overdue and justice must be done to atone for the vulnerability of women in the workplace. But in the chaos of accusations, as happened during the McCarthy Era, it is now equally at risk for a guilt-free man, by simply being accused, to be instantly ruined. The big lie cuts both ways, bloodying those who deny women's vulnerability and those who deny excesses in reaction. Civil service veterans may have lawful protections, but fartworm commissioners with little conscience have easy ways around them.

In this commissioner's case, all his replacement senior leaders in the Department owed their promotions to no one else but him. Moreover, the most prominent of his replacement leaders came from out-of-state, which of itself raises some interesting questions. People who flip flop from State to State looking for advancement may be suspiciously incapable of sustaining a long term relationship, whereas it speaks volumes about a leader who wins a solid reputation over long years with the same people. On the other hand, people who bounce from state to state may simply be looking for advancement, or they may be abandoning professional mistakes and broken trusts behind them. In any case, they have invested heavily in this new opportunity by uprooting their families and children and moving them to a completely new state where their kids start school again not knowing anyone and the spouse has to find a new job too. When this happens, these new transferees are particularly vulnerable. They dare not make waves in the new place, giving the commissioner even more than usual power over them. In this particular instance, the commissioner had in effect brilliantly cemented all loyalty to himself at the expense of staff diversity, vast stores of lost institutional knowledge...and human carnage...within the supposedly protected ranks of civil service. The result was a rupturing of the continuity of the agency's programs and services. The institutional brain trust had vanished.

Such behavior from a commissioner would seem to bleed into the sands of sociopathy, for it makes some weird sort of Machiavellian sense that when there's rapid turnover of senior leaders, the organization becomes confused and disorganized. Consummation of power bereft of challenge in an unstable environment. But it is also a usurpation of the spirit of civil service.

And that's how welfare leadership works.

CHAPTER 14

Having a Civil Service Does Not Necessarily Translate into A Good Service

Civil servants in my experience have impressed me as highly committed public employees, by and large. That doesn't mean, though, they've been taught how to do their jobs or have been chosen because they know the job.

That includes my own fartworm self.

Here's the first example of monkey phlegm in government administration that I encountered in my career in State government. It was I. My first management position was taking charge of the New Hampshire Food Stamp Program, where I discovered my job description was strictly limited to a) writing excuses for New Hampshire's high payment error rate; b) tracking loss of food stamp coupons (when we still had them) in the postal system; c) writing annual and semi-annual reports to the feds about ethnicity of recipients and the like; and d) writing policy to put in the standard operating procedure manual for eligibility workers to follow when they determined whether an applicant could receive food stamps. Everything the food stamp program manager in New Hampshire did was designed to jump through one of these federal hoops.

Let's just keep the wheels turning.

There's a metaphor for this. It's the simple handshake. People are taught to look confident and gaze into the other person's eyes when they shake hands. Sincere people in the business world want desperately to show they've learned the protocol so I can't count the number of times people have been so intent on looking me in the eye that they miss my hand and squeeze my fingers instead, or the clasp goes completely amiss. Except that it busts conventional wisdom, there's nothing wrong with keeping your eyes on the hands to get it right, then looking confidently up into the other person's eyes.

People though can tend to jump through hoops intent on appearing correct instead of focusing on the actual job to be done.

It took me a while to figure out that I was myself a fartworm jumping through the wrong hoops. But eventually it did occur to me to ask the inconvenient question.

"Why do we have a food stamp program?"

It seems so simple now, of course. The question, that is. What is not simple in government is getting workers to step outside themselves to ask that inconvenient question about their job. Why? Because it's the most dangerous thing in government in terms of service and career. These are no longer colonial volunteers and churchmen running welfare. Like everyone else, almost all civil servants are ambitious and want to be recognized with a promotion. When they do, they much too often think they're successful if they simply keep the wheels turning. Write up those federal reports. Art up some attractive cover pages. Do up some impressive, mind-numbing PowerPoints and deliver them confidently in front of a crowd where all eyes are on you. Speak with authority. Make the excuses for the high error rate look believable, never mind fixing the error rate problem because everyone agrees it can't be fixed. The gaudier the wheels as they keep turning, the more everyone is self-congratulatory on the shiny bauble of their program.

Unfortunately it's more complicated than that.

When I had that epiphanic moment—it was 1998—and asked myself, "Why do we have a food stamp program," I was thunderstruck to realize that the question had not been asked for a long, long time, not even at the federal level. Since 1975 the program simply "was" because federal law said it was supposed to be. Food stamp program managers in New Hampshire had been going through the motions, churning out benefits, jumping through hoops, keeping the wheels turning.

So why do we have a food stamp program? The question was the hard part. The answer was easy. "The food stamp program exists as a nutritional safety net for impoverished people." And there was no escaping the follow-up question. "Well, if the food stamp program is a nutritional safety net, how well is it working in New Hampshire?"

Questions can be dangerous. It is why people avoid them, because, as one good friend with whom I worked over the years was fond of stating, "If you ask it, you own it."

So I figured it out. We actually had no idea whether the program was making a difference in New Hampshire as a nutritional safety net that prevented hunger. Everyone from Congress, the USDA, and on down to state administrators assumed the food stamp program was working (just as they now assume the TANF Program is working). Or maybe more accurately, they assumed that since they had made the program *available* to impoverished people and pumped out food stamp coupons, their responsibility in the whole thing was done. It was up to impoverished people to apply or not, right? You can lead a horse to water? Or more exactly, you can create the water, the horse is on its own.

After that moment and for the next two weeks I put everything else aside and investigated Census data comparing the number of people on food stamps to the number of New Hampshire residents in poverty. It was startling. First, according to my estimates about 42% of eligible people in New Hampshire actually participated in the Food Stamp program. That is a pretty awful market share when the "business" is a monopoly. Second, the likelihood of people participating was linked to age. Families with children aged zero to five years were about three times more likely to participate than seniors over age sixty. In fact, the participation rate of impoverished seniors in the program was only 20% to 25%.

In short, asking the inconvenient question led to the awkward realization that New Hampshire's nutritional safety net wasn't working very well. People in New Hampshire were going to bed hungry. Oh, the wheels were turning all right. Apart from federal penalties for the error rate, we looked good enough. But my research showed we were definitely not meeting muster if the true goal was to fight hunger in our State.

I put all this research into my Outreach Plan for 1999, when very few states had one, and shipped it off to the USDA feds. (I did put an attractive, artful cover on it.) Apparently it got noticed because a year or two later the feds centralized doing participation rate analyses for every state, and USDA made participation rates a national performance measure from then on. Eventually the outreach program I put into place brought New Hampshire's participation rate up to 85%, which is about average for the nation these days. In 2002, New Hampshire won a $1 million TANF High Performance Bonus because the outreach program was a national leader at increasing the participation of children in food stamps.

As I said, though, asking the inconvenient question is a risk. Most often it begins with initial resistance from other workers who think our handle on the business is already adequate, so resent any extra work the question brings them. In this instance, I worked for a Supervisor who was both brilliant and supportive. She let me do it.

But there is another risk. Change has to go through leadership in the inner circle.

To initiate the outreach effort for food stamps, I created a poster. Easy enough, since I had worked doing newspaper advertising in college. My poster's layout centered on a photo of two little girls about nine and ten years old. They were sisters and had their arms wrapped around each other's shoulders as they smiled sweetly, yet with innocent mischief, into the camera.

I worked out a caption for it: "Even little angels need nutrition." Underneath that in smaller print, was *The Food Stamp Program* followed by contact information.

When I had the mock-up done, I took it upstairs to get permission to print and distribute. I had to convince two levels of leadership, the Division Director (a guy who had the job before I did) and an Associate Commissioner. Thankfully, they too were supportive about Outreach and even the concept of a poster, but they shook their heads skeptically at the caption. "We can't use the word "angels," they nodded solemnly to each other. "That's too religious."

So fine. I changed the caption to read "Food Stamps: because our biggest gifts come in our smallest packages." That one passed muster with my bosses, but there was one more step.

They said I had to take it to the commissioner.

Now this particular commissioner was a dyed in the wool hard core conservative. He was notorious for being rude to people, dismissing them with a wave of his hand or, worse, signaling the meeting was over by abruptly turning his back on people to work at his computer. Most everyone was afraid of him.

I dragged into the commissioner's office. I'd heard he was always all business, so I launched into it right away. I told him about my food stamp research and my recommendation that we do outreach. And I was honest. I admitted to him that I was looking to increase the number of people on welfare. Then I waited to be fired...or at least for him to wave his hand shooing me out of his office. Thing is, the picture of those two little girls was so darned cute, that when I pulled it out and handed it to him, he immediately smiled. And about increasing the food stamp caseload? He astonished me, saying, "For crying out loud, it's free federal money." He was a great commissioner. He had bought into the Department's mission, listened to me, and made decisions like this one that would cause him to do some explaining to his conservative friends around the State. But he didn't flinch.

Just keeping the wheels turning cannot be allowed to be enough. Over the years I raised other food stamp questions. Why wasn't the internet being allowed as an income deduction for determining food stamp eligibility? People needed it to get jobs in today's world, right? And why can't certain child care costs be an income deduction? Why can't women in a State prison halfway house be eligible for food stamps? After all, they are required to pay rent, buy food, and work in the community. And why can't we take food stamp applications from foster care kids—and give them employment services—*before* they aged out and were statistically likely to become homeless and exposed to addictions? Most of these were all national firsts, or what the

USDA feds called "novel waivers." I asked for them and got them. Now the program wheels weren't just turning, we were actually getting somewhere.

Civil servants can make a difference. Many—hopefully most—of us get in the welfare business to do just that. The dynamics of civil service are overwhelmingly inspiring. It's not so simple as people contracting with government to work eight hours for pay. Rather for most civil servants it is a covenant, a contract of mutual faith. Since the human service agency is charged with helping disadvantaged citizens, when it hires an employee it is in essence asking that employee to embody caring values to the community on behalf of the organization. As for the employee? In my experience, civil service employees working in welfare either want the job in the first place because they are passionate about the same values as the agency, or they come to that passion later, despite that a personal values assessment is rarely a part of the interview process. Good news is, we can usually trust civil servants to get it right as long as their leaders don't get in the way.

The second protection is this.

This is America.

While we should all of us be thinking of ourselves as World citizens, there's no mistaking that the United States was founded on decidedly strong democratic principles by men of honor and integrity. These were men who had deep understanding of aristocratic fartworms and how to keep them in check. They built the legislative, executive and judicial branches to keep a suspicious eye on each other. America's founders knew there would be career fartworms growing massively fat in each branch of government, but at least each fartworm would be competing against every other fartworm in a multi-political party system, always undulating in their political tunnels to bring each other down, to pour copious salt onto the other's slime. Such competition may result in gridlock, but the alternative is worse.

Perhaps the best thing, though, that our founding fathers did, was pave the way for a fourth branch of government: the press. In America, like our democratic allies, the press has permission to investigate the innermost workings of our government. They are the ones responsible to tell us all the truth—all of it, hideous though it may be—and to keep on telling us the truth until it reaches such a critical mass that we can no longer justify defending our status quo. The press has lost their way in recent years, to be sure, and many who call themselves journalists are truly just hack essayists telling factions of us what we want to hear so we can continue with Systems Justification, protecting our *status quo*. But ultimately in America the truth is available, and it will win out. The press will find the bad guys. It won't be perfect, but compare us to Russia and it's easy to figure out.

There is hope for welfare in America. It's handled badly, to be sure, by some managers and leaders in it for egos and ambition. And there's room for improvement, such as a less political selection process for government leaders, strong work requirements on welfare clients and better supports for the safety and well-being of welfare children. Congressman Paul Ryan had the right idea. There are vastly too many programs and overlapping services for low income people. These need to be consolidated both as a cost saver and a government efficiency, and so people in need can navigate the welfare system more easily. The answer, though, is decidedly *not* to block grant the responsibility from the federal government to state governments where the number of fartworms in the way of efficient government increases exponentially. We've seen in TANF that that doesn't work, as States divert welfare money to meet other budget needs. Even food stamps has major issues despite it being a federal program without fifty -two different State permutations. Block granting food stamps to states is not a solution, but an evasion of accountability. You can't write a poem by committee.

Maybe…maybe the hardest thing in human nature…is making part of life about someone else…every day…every hour…every moment that counts. Maybe it's unfair to be so harshly critical of leaders in welfare when they don't do that. But then again, some do. And if they can, it should be okay to expect better of them all.

It is a carnivorous world. We—all of us—have a choice. Either you live life with conviction, or you wind up a sycophantic chump to people with more ambition than character. So believe in something. Step outside yourselves for a moment and ask the inconvenient question. The truth is available if you're willing to listen to yourself over others, go find the evidence, and then go the distance. And of course…

…Go vote.

APPENDIX A

History of Food Stamp Program:

The political debate in America and New Hampshire
(1805 to 2000)

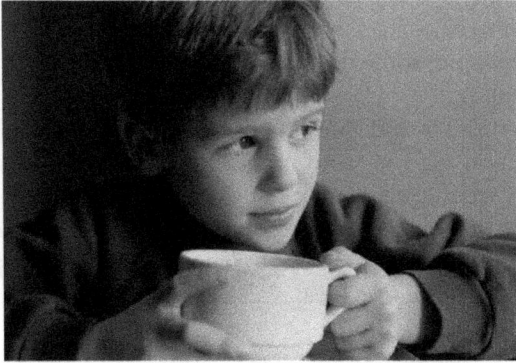

For a social program administered by the federal government with such an ostensibly good cause, the Food Stamp Program is not without controversy. It is, in fact, plagued with the very controversy that rests at the heart of America's historical debate regarding the ownership of assistance programs to aid the nation's needy. And it is true, moreover, that it is necessary to thoroughly understand the nature of this debate, since it rages around us today, and has implications for the future of the New Hampshire Food Stamp Program as the Food Stamp Act moves toward reauthorization in two years.

No time in history is more illustrative of the debate about where to place the nation's safety net against hunger, than the events occurring subsequent to the stock market crash of 1929. This crash precipitated the beginning of a depression that lasted over ten years, with a devastation of human suffering that stunned the nation. By January of 1930, about 5 million Americans were unemployed and unable to purchase sufficient food. By the time Franklin Roosevelt took office in early 1933, unemployment had risen to an estimated 15 million people. At the same time, wages paid to those remaining in the workforce had dropped by a third. Banks closed permanently, separating many families from their life savings–their own personal safety net against hunger. Countless families lost their homes because they couldn't pay their mortgage, or sold them at substantial loss so they could buy food, since cities would generally not give relief to anyone who owned a home. People slept in culverts, fields, cars, or thrown -together tin shacks. Most of all, there was hunger. Malnourishment sapped the energy of children, and made grown men unable to work even when they could find it (Komisar, 1974, p. 44).

But what was government doing? –It was doing what it had always done. Presiding over the first two and a half years of the Depression, Herbert Hoover orchestrated no direct relief for the nation's starving, unemployed people, for he was paralyzed by a tradition of minimalistic federal government he had inherited from Thomas Jefferson.

The debate about welfare really begins with Jefferson, who believed in an un-centralized government, which is, of course, the antithesis of the monarchy against which the American Revolution was fought. But there was something else, and to understand it we must visualize the America of 1804 over which Jefferson presided as President. The economy was agrarian, and the original thirteen colonies were still sparsely settled, so opportunity for new farms abounded. Moreover, opportunity of staggering proportions had just opened up with the Louisiana Purchase, whereby millions of acres of uninhabited land became available for clearing and planting. Thomas Jefferson, with good reason, believed the undeveloped America of 1804 was an agrarian society of such extent, it was unimaginable that every man could not find free or cheap uncultivated land to work, and by the sweat of his brow raise his station in life.

Jefferson's era, then, is the source of the myth that there is an invisible welfare in the New World, that every man has equal opportunity to pull himself up by his own bootstraps, and this myth grew. Fifty years after Jefferson, in the mid-19th century, Franklin Pierce, the President from New Hampshire, vetoed legislation to fund construction of mental institutions, echoing a Jeffersonian sentiment with the words, "I cannot find any authority in the Constitution for making the Federal Government the great almoner of public charity throughout the United States (Jansson, 1997, p. 65)." In his turn, Hoover denied direct federal aid to the needy during the Depression with an echo of Pierce, "You cannot extend the mastery of government over the daily lives of the people without at the same time making it the master of their souls and thoughts (Trattner, 1979, p. 225)."

But America changed in the 130 years between Jefferson and the Depression. America made a transition from a primarily agrarian nation, to an industrial world power. And there was a more subtle change: the skills needed by industrial workers were quite different than those needed by farmers. Industrial workers require skills more reflective of the need to operate within the confines of masses of people working together. They must be able to perform or learn to perform with a quality satisfactory to an employer. Industrial workers must be able to work communally with others, accept supervision, and navigate all the communication byways of modern civilization. This new industrial economy is all very much more socially complicated than the old, Jeffersonian agrarian one. And nothing less than worker survival depends on how well they acquire all these skills, for workers live within not just an industrial economy, but a free enterprise one to boot, one based on the natural price of commodities, which in turn is founded on competition, with the best product reaching the marketplace at the lowest price meeting with the most success. Labor is an economic commodity subject to competition. And competition, by its nature, means there will be winners, and those who do not win. But it took the context of mammoth job layoffs and poverty during the Great Depression, for Americans to achieve a critical consciousness relative to the difference between agrarian and industrial economic vulnerability. Farmers were affected by the crash of 1929, of course, but the real victims were industrial workers, 15 million of them.

But Hoover was slow to adapt. He continued to follow the view of all thirty of his Presidential predecessors, that ownership of assistance programs to aid the nation's needy belonged with charitable, faith and local communities, and not the federal government. However, if this were to be the case, these private and local institutions were feeble against the onslaught of misery that marked the Great Depression. The American Friends Service Committee providing relief in the coal producing communities of West Virginia and Kentucky developed a stratagem for coping: namely, they weighed children and refused food to those whose body weight was not yet 10% less than it ought to be; nonetheless they quickly exhausted their inadequate funds (Komisar, 1974, p.48). At the same time, the chairman of the Red Cross, John Barton Payne, spoke out against a bill that would have provided $25 million for relief because it would perhaps adversely affect his own Red Cross fundraising. He said, "Why should the Government be dealing in this sort of thing when the people have plenty of money?" (Komisar, 1974, p.45). Other proposals for meeting the hunger problem without government involvement were flatly unrealistic and insensitive. A member of Hoover's own cabinet proposed that restaurants ought to preserve their leftovers to give to the poor—with, of course, the suggestion that patrons should be requested not to drop cigar or cigarette ashes in the food. As it turned out, this was both a meaningless proposal and sensible advice, since in Chicago crowds of people, including children, already waited for garbage trucks to dump their load, before digging into the mounds of refuse with sticks to mine food scraps. (Trattner, 1979, p. 228)

The magnitude of suffering during the Depression stunned the nation, and out of this arose a view that opposed minimalism of federal government: that is, a debate. It wasn't until after three hard winters of the Depression and ineffectual relief from the charitable and local communities, that the American people's increasingly loud demand for federal action–even talk of revolution (Trattner, 1979, p.228; Komisar, 1974, p.48)–could no longer be denied by Hoover, and he signed the Emergency Relief and Construction Act in the summer of 1932 just six months after he had vetoed similar legislation. This law was also ineffectual and riddled with patronage. It was designed to provide government aid to large corporations and banks, and to lend money to states so the states could provide more effective direct relief to the poor. It provided a funding level of $ 300 million, but by the end of 1932 it had only loaned 10% for the purpose of direct relief, largely due to fact that loans would have fallen due in just three years, in the summer of 1935 (Komisar, 1974, p. 49). Moreover, there were irregularities associated with the funding. One Chicago bank headed by former Vice President Charles G. Dawes–who was, in hindsight, conflicted since he was also head of the agency distributing these federal loans–received over 30% of the $300 million. (Trattner, 1979, p.226 *n*)

This legislation was not the response the American people were looking for, and Hoover stubbornly resisted other opportunities to provide hunger relief. For the first three Depression era winters, 60 thousand bushels of surplus wheat were held in federal warehouse storage, rather than being distributed to the nation's starving unemployed (Komisar, 1974, p.47). But the most insidious example of the inadequacy of Hoover's position on the debate as to ownership of direct relief, came in 1930 when he approved $ 45 million to feed Arkansas livestock, but simultaneously refused $25 million to feed the farmers themselves (Trattner, 1979, p.225). The Secretary of Agriculture voiced Hoover's side of the debate by stating that money to feed the farmers and their families would "constitute a dangerous step toward the dole system in this country (Komisar, 1974, p.47-8)." Yet at the same time, $2 billion had recently been provided to assist business interests–banks, railroads, insurance companies, industry–, causing one Senator, Robert LaFollette, to speculate ironically whether the $2 billion would have the side effect of dampening the entrepreneurial spirit of these businessmen in the same way that Hoover worried direct relief would end the initiative of the unemployed to work. But Hoover wasn't destined to be the principle worrier for much longer. Concerned citizens were marching on Washington. Instead of greeting them with action, he turned them away with soldiers (Komisar, 1974, p.49).

The Great Depression spawned a new intolerance for Hoover's insistence on a small federal government with a balanced budget regardless the cost in human suffering, and into the vacuum of the people's impatience with Hoover's inaction, sprang the first meaningful debate about the ownership of assistance programs for the needy. Franklin Roosevelt campaigned for election to the Presidency on the promise that he would utilize the powers of the Presidency to *do* something about the needs of people, including hunger. After he became President, he was true to his word. Almost immediately, he signed the Federal Emergency Relief Act, and with a stroke of the pen legitimized and institutionalized a view of the role of federal government in the welfare of the nation's citizens, that was unique from any President that came before him. Under this legislation, money wasn't loaned to states, but given on a matching basis. The majority of this aid was distributed by state and local governments to needy people as food relief.

In 1935, Roosevelt prompted enactment of legislation that allowed the Department of Agriculture to purchase surplus farm commodities and use them to provide direct food assistance ("From Farm to Table," 1998) This marked the first federal involvement in a nutritional assistance program, and is the great-grandparent of the Food Stamp Program. The federal organization established for the distribution of surplus food through public and private agencies was called the Federal Surplus Relief Corporation. Basic staples were provided, including flour, cheese, cereal, apples, potatoes, and butter. In addition, blankets made from surplus cotton were provided. These supplies were given out through State administered warehouses, where destitute people often waited for hours to claim their food. Furthermore, presence at these distribution sites was stigmatizing, for it clearly segregated recipients from the mainstream population at a time when the Hoover view of relief continued to be a major presence in people's emotional, if not intellectual, view of welfare. When the federal administrator of the program, Harry Hopkins, ended the warehouse distribution sites, he said, "It is a matter of opinion whether more damage is done to the human spirit by a lack of vitamins or complete surrender of choice." (Komisar, 1974, p. 51).

In 1939, federal nutrition program administrators proved they had gotten the hang of program administration. Instead of requiring recipients to visit distribution sites for direct food delivery, they established a method of benefit issuance that relied on a special currency: stamps. People who qualified purchased orange stamps equal to what they normally spent on groceries. As a supplement, they were also provided at no extra cost a blue stamp worth fifty cents for every dollar in orange stamps they bought. Then, the recipient took the orange stamps to the grocery store and bought whatever foods they chose. The blue stamps, however, were relegated only for certain eligible surplus foods, including butter, eggs, some meats, flour, and dry beans (USDA News, 1999). This method had advantages. It ended the one stigma of visiting the surplus food warehouses. There were still stigmatizing issues, however, for stamps were visible to the mainstream community in grocery stores. But there was also no waiting in long lines, and people could now take away an amount of food they could safely store–in an era when refrigeration was comprised of iceboxes, if people had them–and come back for more at their convenience. And, parenthetically, this is why the Food Stamp Program is called the Food Stamp Program, even after benefit currency stopped being stamps in 1943, when the program was suspended during WWII because there were no surplus foods to distribute and unemployment was no longer a national dilemma. And even after benefits became coupons, not stamps. And even now, when half the nation has converted to electronic debit issuance system, benefits are still called food stamps.

It must be clarified, however, that the presence of a surplus food program did not automatically signal the end of hunger in America during the Depression. On the contrary, in 1939 when nearly a sixth of the population depended on relief, hunger continued to victimize America's poor. One state provided food benefits that were about a fifth of a minimum standard food budget. When Ohio ran out of money for food distribution, the governor refused to call a special session to provide more matching money, and the state also denied cities permission to raise taxes to provide relief on their own. In Chicago, food benefits were two thirds of the minimum standard food budget, and so many children were weakened from malnourishment, a community center stopped offering active sports like basketball. Over half of states gave nothing or next to nothing in food to people thought to be employable (much like today's ABAWD standards that came out of 1996 welfare reform legislation). A local relief director in New Jersey got extra money only after he convinced officials that it cost more money to bury people than to feed them. In Omaha, it was reported that some children were too hungry to go to school (Komisar, 1974, p.69). And when World War II broke out, some men drafted for the military were pronounced unfit for duty due to malnourishment ("From Farm to Table," 1998, p. 49).

American agriculture was once again producing surpluses after the War, and in 1949, to prevent waste, the Secretary of Agriculture was directed to ensure that commodities collected through federal price support purchases, be distributed to low-income people. The first purpose, then, of the post-war era's nutritional safety net, was to purchase farm surpluses; by reducing the number of commodities on the market, according to the laws of supply and demand, the prices were stabilized. The second purpose was to prevent waste. It was by natural extension, but not primary intent, that the third purpose was to meet the nutritional needs of the nation's poor (Trattner, 1979, p.257). Nor was this a new sense of prioritizing. The motivating factor behind the federal surplus food program established in 1935, was primarily to shore up the agricultural economy (Komisar, 1974, p.51), which had been depressed throughout the 1920's (Jansson, 1997, p.150). Yet, still remembering the poverty of the 1930's, Congress authorized President Eisenhower to reinstate a nutritional safety net. Eisenhower refused the opportunity, but in 1961 Kennedy established a pilot program ("From Farm to Table," 1998, p.49). The pendulum of the debate had swung twice. But ultimately it was a coalition that established the Food Stamp Program, and American farmers played a major role.

The problem with the surplus food program, was that it was dependent on the type of foods that were grown in surplus rather than linked to the nutritional needs of the nation's poor. By passing the Food Stamp Act in 1964, Congress gave choice to recipients by expanding what foods they could buy. The list of eligible foods that marked the surplus food program, was eliminated in favor of a system wherein recipients were enabled to purchase whatever foods they chose. As in 1939, people purchased stamps before going to the grocery market, at a cost of about 66 cents per dollar value in the market. While this first Food Stamp Act represented major positive movement forward on behalf of the poor, it also retained some of the disadvantages inherent in the surplus food system. Firstly, it ignored the needs of people who had zero income with which to purchase stamps in the first place, so the poorest of the poor, those who needed the nutritional safety net most, were blocked from access. Secondly, use of stamps in the grocery market instead of cash continued to stigmatize recipients by segregating them from the general community, which also served as a disincentive blocking access to participation for many. Thirdly, states were allowed to establish their own eligibility criteria, so income levels for participation, for instance, differed widely. And fourthly, the 1964 Act strode the fence in the debate about the ownership of nutritional assistance: it made the Food Stamp Program optional for states, and only twenty-two states participated (Schmulowitz, 1994).

Leading up to 1964, the coalition that supported the surplus food program in 1935 was growing stronger. At the beginning of the surplus food program, the nation was in the throes of the Depression, and a critical consciousness about hunger brought the middle class into support of centralized nutritional assistance, and national advocacy groups formed. Also, as has been mentioned, agricultural interests benefited from the price supports that went along with the Department of Agriculture's purchase of their excess farm commodities, stabilizing market prices. In 1939, when government started selling stamps for use in grocery stores in lieu of warehouse distribution sites, grocery retailers also began to see the benefit of a federal budget dedicated to purchases in their markets. The Food Stamp Act of 1964 did not change the coalition. The only distinction for farmers was the opening up of their market beyond a list of eligible surplus food to include the entire base of their product; this, if anything, expanded their support for the Food Stamp Program. Interestingly, Bob Dole, a Congressman from Kansas in 1964, voted against the Food Stamp Act when it came up in the House Agriculture Committee, but later, influenced by farm interests in his state, led a coalition in Congress that promoted the Food Stamp Program ("From Farm to Table," 1998, p.49). It is not surprising, then, that the first paragraph of the Food Stamp Act reads:

AN ACT

To strengthen the agricultural economy; to help to achieve a fuller and more effective use of food abundances; to provide for improved levels of nutrition among low-income households through a cooperative Federal-State program of food assistance to be operated through normal channels of trade; and for other purposes.

The debate over the ownership of the nutritional safety net continued in the 1970's with some rather sharp swerves from the Nixon Administration. First, in 1971, the Department of Agriculture pronounced more restrictive eligibility requirements and fewer benefits for food stamp recipients. The National Welfare Rights Organization sued, and Nixon backed off on his policy. Instead, surprisingly he signed legislation in 1971 that raised benefits and tied them to cost of living so they remained stable relative to the economy (Komisar, 1974, p.115). The legislation also established national eligibility criteria, provided free food stamps for people who couldn't afford to purchase them, and established work requirements for participation. But the biggest change came in 1973, when supporters of the national nutritional safety net won their largest victory in the debate since establishment of Roosevelt's surplus food program, for the legislation *mandated* the Food Stamp Program in all states. As disincentives for refusal to comply, the legislation provided for Medicaid funding penalties and phased out the Depression era surplus food program as disincentives for recalcitrant states. And New Hampshire was the most recalcitrant of all the states.

There is no better example of the continued liveliness of the debate over ownership of nutrition assistance, than in New Hampshire, which argued the issue longer than any other State and required a special session of the legislature to resolve (Higgins, 3/27/74). New Hampshire's opposition was led by Governor Meldrim Thomson, who proposed an alternative county-based food voucher system that would have cost the state $2.5 million, instead of the federally subsidized version that would cost $1.75 million. So, even if we are to disregard Medicaid penalties, the administrative cost for state independence from centralization of the nutritional safety net was to be $750,000 per year, and that side of the debate still had advocates. Nevertheless, Thompson's plan was not mentioned by members of the New Hampshire House when they passed approval of the Food Stamp Program on March 7, 1974 (Norris, 3/7/74). The bill was to replace New Hampshire's surplus food program when it expired on June 30th. Ironically, June, 1974, was also the month in which the story that impoverished elders were resorting to eating dog and cat food appeared in a report to a Senate committee hearing on nutrition; the story was undocumented, however, and has since been discredited (Johnston, 11/26/74), but not without first casting yet another shadow on the anti-centralized safety net side of the debate. A perceived problem is still a problem.

Governor Thomson compromised by urging the Senate, which had yet to consider the bill, to place responsibility for creating policy and administering the program in the hands of the Governor and Council instead of the Division of Welfare (Paul, 3/20/74). However, a top Washington administrator for the Food Stamp Program telephoned Senator C. Robertson Trowbridge, chairman of the Finance Committee, to assure New Hampshire that Governor Thomson's proposal was unacceptable, and on March 21st, the Finance Committee voted to approve the House version of the food stamp plan intact and send it to the Senate floor, regardless of a clear hint from the Governor that he would veto the legislation. (Paul, 3/22/74). On March 26th, the full Senate approved the House version of the food stamp bill, and sent it to the Governor for signature.

But Governor Thomson wasn't done. That same day, he denounced Senator Trowbridge for his "flagrant and careless manipulation of the truth," and cited a telegram he received the previous day from another Department of Agriculture official to the effect that the Governor's plan to house the Food Stamp Program under the authority of Governor and Council was "not in conflict with federal food stamp regulations." But the Governor's federal contact was not a top Washington official, and Trowbridge responded, "It's typical of the Thomson administration that when they get a no answer from one federal official that they go out and find a lower, unsuspecting federal official who will somehow say what they want (Higgins, 3/27/74, pages 1 and 16). Finally, on April 1st, the Food Stamp Program passed into law without Thompson's signature. The Governor cited that his reason for not vetoing the legislation was that the bill had been the primary reason for the special legislative session ("Thomson Allows Food Stamp Passage," 4/2/74). More likely, however, was that he knew the legislature had the votes to override his veto.

The debate about the Food Stamp Program has continued to the present. But it's a different debate than in the past, although it remains traditional for political rhetoricians to resurrect the myth of American welfare, that anyone can raise himself up by his own bootstraps with a little sweat and hard work. Yet the purpose is usually no longer to eradicate nutritional assistance from federal programs, but to limit it. For now the debate is no longer about the advisability of federal ownership of assistance programs for the needy.

Critical consciousness about the necessity for that has long since become a standardized norm. Instead, the modern debate in Food Stamps has to do with the very real issue of welfare as a "growth industry."

To understand the new debate is to admit that, although history may look querulously at Governor Meldrim Thompson's opposition to the fostering of the Food Stamp Program in New Hampshire, he also was a forerunner at drawing attention to something critically essential to understanding the management of government assistance programs.

Until the early 1930's, services to low-income people were delivered by volunteers in churches, charities, and towns, volunteers with nothing to gain themselves. But spokespersons for a modern view of the old debate assert that the motivation of service delivery people changed when they began working for government, drawing paychecks, receiving benefit packages, and becoming careerists, so that now people delivering services have a personal, not just moral, stake in the perpetuation of the programs they deliver. Adherents of this side of the debate worry that there is a creeping tendency for programs to become more costly as government becomes a "growth industry," protecting its self-interest: the more complicated service programs become, or the more money funded to them, the more secure are the governmental service providers' careers. Clearly, the debate in Congress today around welfare generally, and Food Stamps specifically, is more about welfare as a growth industry, than whether the federal government should be involved in the first place. This would seem to be a wise budgetary-based debate to have.

In some instances, this debate has been silently voiced. For instance, the resource test for eligibility—that is, how much in cashable assets an applicant may have—has been $2,000 since 1974, regardless of annual inflation. In addition, it was established in 1974 that the fair market value (not equity value) of vehicles above $4,500 would count toward this resource limit. In twenty-five years, this vehicle resource limit has risen by only $150, causing more individuals to be ineligible due to resources each year. Had the vehicle threshold been responsive to an average 3% inflation per year, in today's dollars the threshold would be $8,000 instead of $4,650. Then, in 2000, Congress partially addressed this inequity in food stamp eligibility (one cannot eat a car), with legislation allowing states the option to use their TANF vehicle resource policy for food stamps beginning July 1, 2001.

In other instances, the debate over the nation's nutritional safety net has been more loudly voiced. In 1982, the Reagan Administration managed to elicit passage of the Omnibus Reconciliation Act, which is credited with reducing the Food Stamp Program enrollment by one million people (Jansson, 1997, p.278). Among other things, it created tighter disability definitions, prorated benefits in the first month, established the gross income test, and prohibited boarders and strikers from participating. But in 1985, proponents of the program made gains during the reauthorization of the Food Stamp Act They regained looser disability definitions, made recipients of AFDC and SSI automatically income and resource eligible, and increased deductions for earned income, child care and excess shelter. Also, although the Food Stamp bill of 1971 established the first work registration requirement on recipients, it was in 1985 that all states were mandated to implement employment and training programs as a part of food stamp administration.

Program debate continued to eventuate in legislation that caused the program to seesaw. In 1996, major cutbacks were pronounced in welfare reform legislation (Personal Responsibility and Work Opportunity Act, or PRWORA), wherein for the first time certain subsets of the American population were restricted access to the program. Non-citizens were rendered ineligible for allotted time periods, and could become eligible only after earning forty quarters of Social Security earnings. Able-bodied adults without dependents (ABAWDS)–that is, individuals 18 to 50 without children or disabilities–were restricted to just three months of participation unless they met an average of twenty hours per week of work each month. States were also given the option to prohibit program access to convicted drug felons. In yet another insidious cutback, the personal exemption allowance was frozen at 1996 levels, and may no longer be increased due to cost of living. PRWORA was candid in its approach to the debate: it meant to save $26 billion dollars over the course of the seven year lifespan of the legislation, which also happened to be the existing annual budget for the program. PRWORA contained other restrictions as well, but as a voice in the ongoing debate about program growth, it did not go long without being answered by the opposition.

The coalition of Republicans led by Newt Gingrich which succeeded with passage of PWRORA disintegrated to some degree, and the Clinton Administration was able to ameliorate the impact of the legislation. In 1997, the Budget Reconciliation Act loosened some of the restrictions on aliens, and provided substantial funds for states to create employment and training programs to allow ABAWDS to maintain eligibility. (New Hampshire was the first state in the Northeast to design and implement such a program.) In addition, the Department of Agriculture adopted an interpretive twist to the vehicle resource policy, allowing states waivers to exempt a vehicle under existing "inaccessible" resource policy if the owner has one-half or less in equity value. Then, taking this even farther, as stated elsewhere here, legislation passed to allow states to adopt their TANF vehicle resource policy for food stamps, if it is more lenient that existing food stamp policy.

The debate continues to be lively. In 1996, the State of Texas, then under the governorship of George W. Bush, attempted to privatize the Food Stamp Program. Only through the direct intervention of the President was the initiative defeated. While the Food Stamp Program was not mentioned meaningfully in the Bush/Gore campaign of 2000, ramifications of Bush's election are potentially significant. If Texas were to reiterate its attempt to privatize food stamps, a precedent setting decision would have to be made by a President whose power base is in Texas. Less speculatively, the Food Stamp Act is due for reauthorization in 2002. Positioning for the legislative effort, the Department of Agriculture has attempted to restructure the image of the program from one of fraud and abuse, to one of hunger prevention, by developing a Strategic Plan with the fight against hunger as the principal mission, by encouraging states to develop outreach plans (only nine states had one in 1999, New Hampshire being one), and by conducting national reviews of program access, to ensure that states are not restricting access to the needy. The specific issues that will emerge in the debate about program growth are not yet clear, but one thing is certain, the period leading into the reauthorization of the Food Stamp Act in 2002 will be marked by yet another shift in the pendulum.

BIBLIOGRAPHY

Komisar, L. (1974). *Down and Out in the USA: a history of social welfare.* New York: New Viewpoints.

Jansson, B. (1997). *The Reluctant Welfare State: American social welfare policies-- past, present, future (3rd ed.).* Pacific Grove: Brooks/Cole Publishing Company.

Trattner, W. (1979). *From Poor Law to Welfare State: a history of social welfare in America (2nd ed.).* New York: The Free Press.

Rossi, P. (1998). *Feeding the Poor: assessing federal food aid.* Washington, D.C.: The AEI Press.

From Farm to Table. (1998, September). *Government Executive,* p. 49.

U.S. Department of Agriculture. (1999, July-August). *USDA News,* pp. 2-3. Retrieved June 25, 2000 from the World Wide Web: usda.gov/news/pubs/ newslett/old/vol58no6/article5.htm.

United States Social Security Administration. (1994). *Social Security Bulletin,* p. 132. Washington, D.C.: U.S. Government Printing Office.

Higgins, A. (1974, March 27). Thomson Gets Food Stamp Bill. *The Concord Monitor,* p. 1 & 16.

Norris, F. (1974, March 7). Welfare Increase, Food Stamps Pass. *The Concord Monitor,* p. 1.

Johnston, L. (1974, November 26). Are Humans Eating Canned Pet Food: the growth of a rumor. *The New York Times,* p. 44.

Paul, R. (1974, March 20). Flat Grant $600,000 Opposed by Thomson. *The Concord Monitor,* p. 12.

Paul, R. (1974, March 22). Food Stamp Change Is Rejected. The Concord Monitor, p. 12.

Thomson Allows Food Stamp Passage. (1974, April 2). *The Concord Monitor,* p. 1.

APPENDIX B

The Welfare Timeline

TANF Work Program History

1935: The Social Security Act passed into law. Among many other programs, it introduced public assistance to dependent children in households headed by single-parents. At this point single parents were mostly widows (Occupational Health and Safety law did not pass until 1970).

1967: Beginning with Lyndon Johnson, a number of Presidents attempted to jumpstart work programs for welfare recipients. These were voluntary on states.

1995: New Hampshire was operating under Ronald Reagan's Job Opportunities and Basic Skills (JOBS) Program. JOBS required single parents on welfare to work or participate in education or job training if their child was over age three. Mandatory clients were required to participate in eight weeks of job search, followed by another eight weeks of job search within a twelve month period (which model was embedded in the Food Stamp work program expectations also). Clients with recent employment were sent to NHES where employment counselors helped place them in jobs. Other clients interested in job training were sent to what are now Workforce Investment Act services. Clients with barriers were sent to DHHS social workers. No work participation rate had been established.

1996: The Personal Responsibility and Work Opportunity Act (welfare reform) mandated work requirements for welfare parents. The law block-granted federal funds to States, created allowable work activities, set minimum participation thresholds, established allowable exemptions, created the mandatory work participation rate targets, and established cash penalties for States that failed to meet those targets. However, states could calculate the amount of reduction to the caseload each year as measured against 1994, and this reduction counted toward the work participation rate. Because 1994 was the peak year for caseload increases caused by the recession then, New Hampshire's subsequent caseload reduction reduced our federal participation target to 8%. With effectively no accountability, New Hampshire was not pressured to implement PRWORA's work activities nor the time limits associated with those activities (such as the six week restriction for job search/job readiness).

2006: The Deficit Reduction Act Reauthorized TANF in February of 2006. The new law changed the caseload reduction credit comparison year to 2005, defined existing work activities, and required states to actually verify work participation hours. Abruptly New Hampshire became accountable. To avoid financial penalty, DFA had seven months to redesign TANF State law and NHEP processes, starting with an examination of where clients were who were not counting toward participation. DFA made the following changes.

- 70% of clients were no-shows at Orientation, after which it took six months to sanction the client who never participated. DFA made Orientation a condition of eligibility. Result: 75% are do-shows.
- 500 new TANF clients entered and another 500 left the program every month. Each new client counted against the participation rate that first month because of the delay in being placed in a countable activity, so DFA developed the Portfolio, a self-directed activity given out at Orientations with instructions to begin work on it as soon as the client received their Notice of Decision opening their case.
- DFA's job readiness contractor was requiring up to six weeks before a client could enter their program. Because of this time lag and because of the time limit on job readiness, DFA lost participation for all these clients.
- 236 clients had been assigned the GED activity for thirty hours in contradiction to Federal requirements which only allow it as a secondary activity for ten hours (except teen parents). When DFA asked the GED contractor (NH Department of Education) to tell us how many clients actually attended the full thirty scheduled hours, they answered *"Half."* DFA eliminated the contract but still allows GED (now called HISET) through existing and free community adult education programs. Clients who don't fulfill hourly requirements get placed into a different activity.
- 400 individuals had been placed into job search for over four consecutive weeks (many had been there for months) in contradiction to federal requirements which limit that activity to six weeks, only four of which can be consecutive (this limit is a combined limit for both job search and job readiness). Now, when job search is appropriate, and when the six week time limit has been used, job search must be an expectation on top of another, countable activity.

- Sanction policies had been ineffective. TANF parents who did not comply with work program requirements were allowed six months of reduced benefits under sanction. Moreover, the full family was not placed in sanction, rather only the offending parent. Federal regulations, however, had established that clients in sanction beyond three months count against the 50% rate. DFA changed sanction policy to reduce the full sanction time frame from six months to ten weeks. Clients may not receive benefits while in sanction beyond three calendar months in a year. Moreover, to curtail what had been a revolving door of clients complying and being reinstated only to re-offend, DFA required that the client participate in good standing for two weeks before restitution of their full benefit.

• 600 Alternative Work Experience (AWEP) sites had been developed with community employers. Most of these had never been filled, costing DFA credibility with employers. Therefore DFA created a business and industry coordinator and contracted with the Community Action Agencies to chart and respond to client work experience needs by community.

• Field Support Managers in charge of Employment Counselors were spending almost all of their time at State Office. One had drifted into being a support services expert working on billing. Another had drifted into being the Heights system advisor. DFA revised these roles to ensure they are in the field every day directly supervising their assigned offices. They have cell phones so they can be reached for questions at any time of the day, even when they're on the road between offices.

• 350 Families with children between the ages of one and two were being exempted from work requirements. DFA made them mandatory.

• About sixty-six families were being exempted due to being pregnant over four months. DFA made them mandatory.

• Individuals were being assigned to the post-secondary education activity much longer than the twelve months maximum allowed by federal law and despite the client hadn't actually taken classes or participated any other way for months. DFA time-limited post-secondary education and ended that practice.

Mere days before the new TANF law was required to be implemented (October 1, 2006) the NHEP Field Administrator terminated her employment. Despite the setback, the program redesign was immensely successful. Under the old program, in September 2006 just 38% of recipients (1577/4055) were assigned to work-related activities. The following month of implementation, October of 2006, this doubled to 72% (2680/3964). The participation rate, which hovered around 13% or less in September, grew to 25.7% *verified* in the very first month of the redesigned program.

On October 15th, two weeks into implementation, the position of Bureau Chief for Welfare was created. As workers got used to their new tools and adapted to the new program design, and as the new Chief, BWW learned the program, participation grew to 50.2% by September of 2007. The TANF team made especially critical improvements in changing the NHEP culture from one of diluted expectations to one of accountabilities. The team also created a strong Verification Plan for reporting of work hours and worked with Heights to create an innovative worker dashboard. Meanwhile, the Business and Industry Coordinator created a strong system for Work Experience Placement development and optimized use of On the Job Training placements.

The US Administration for Children and Families continues to consider New Hampshire a model for how the Deficit Reduction Act should be implemented, and has sent DFA to speak to nearly half of all States on the "Quest for 50%: NH's Moderate Approach." In the five years since implementation, New Hampshire's participation rate has been the highest in the northeast (New England plus New York) three times, and second highest twice.

Precision Case Management

While the Work Participation Rate is the federally mandated outcome measure, and while it is useful as a process indicator of client engagement, it is ultimately not the true measure of success for a TANF Program.

Rather, the true measure of TANF is first how well it serves as a cash safety net for low income children, and second how well it moves those children out of poverty through employment of their parents ... *for the long term*. This latter measure is the full responsibility of the New Hampshire Employment Program (NHEP), not just—and not even primarily—the work participation rate.

Immediately upon adapting TANF to the unmet requirements of 1996 law and the new requirements in the 2006 law, the DFA Director assembled a team in early 2007 with a new purpose: to build a responsible TANF program that balanced firm accountability for clients with adaptive sensitivity to their obstacles to long term independence. The team was comprised of:

- the DFA Director: Terry Smith

- the TANF Program Specialist: Kerry Nelson

- the Child Care Specialist: Janine Lesser

- the TANF Administrator: Lynn Wilder

- the Chief, Bureau of Welfare to Work: Mark Jewell

The goal of this team was twofold. One, it needed to create an evidence-based work program for TANF NHEP that clearly delineated desired outcomes for clients. Two, the team needed to construct a case management continuum that very precisely ensured each outcome was targeted with strategies that were systemically visible, repeatable, and measurable. The term to describe this goal was coined: *Precision Case Management*.

Using a process loosely termed "Back Planning," the team began by identifying outcomes with which TANF recipients should graduate the work program. These outcomes include:

- Employment. Could be survival job, but must be accompanied by clear steps to a career path
- Low likelihood of recidivating
- Barrier coping skills
- Embracing of success instead of fearing it (reduced self-sabotage and psychology of scarcity); includes changing the stigma of TANF
- Post TANF career advancement plan. Plan contents include:
  o Divided Sections
  o Portfolio
  o Summary Sheet for each section
  o Back up permanent record (Electronic EP)
  o Summarize each section (Electronic EP)
  o FAQ's from PowerPoint
  o List of Resources/Phone numbers/Services

☐Mentorships: who to call in an emergency (Call counselor before quitting)

☐Emergency Assistance

☐Monthly summary sheet to go over with the client.

☐Steps from survival to career job

☐Local community etc.

☐Family surroundings and strengthen relationships, possible into to Portfolio

☐Financial management resources in community

☐Childcare R&R from Assistance Handbook

☐Post TANF Plan (PTP)

☐ Tax Prep-research list, include in EITC mailing

☐Medicaid

☐ Form 890, EMA Quarterly Report

☐ Medical travel reimbursement

☐ Extended Food Stamps from Assistance Handbook PTP

☐ School Breakfast/Lunch in from Assistance Handbook PTP

☐ WIC, etc. from Assistance Handbook PTP

☐ Cap Program from Assistance Handbook PTP

☐ Heat and Fuel and Weatherization from Assistance Handbook PTP

☐ Child support-benefits of having state go after child support –outstanding

☐ Rental Guarantee Program (since obsoleted)

- How to conduct an independent job search
- Client Notes section (for them to put in additional information as they collect it)
- Planning client calendar
- Critical documents such as resumes and letters of references (Client file as backup). Post TANF Employment Portfolio

☐ Resume

☐ References

☐ Letters Of Recommendation

☐ Transcripts

☐ Sample of work or certificates

☐ Employer list for career paths in local labor markets

- Shelter (Homelessness prevention)
- Transportation (Good News Garage/other)
- Understanding responsible tenancy
- Possess adequate clothing, esp. appropriate work wear
- Worker check list for each interview
- Action list to success (i.e. Child Specific resources) – Dealing with "personal baggage" that might prevent from moving forward in career track
- Nutrition Education
- Financial literacy
- EITC / Childcare credit
- Credit Emergency Assistance
- Predatory Lending
- Child support-benefits of having state go after child support outstanding
- Checking Management
- Debt Management

- Budget Management
- IDA
- Landlord/Tenant Relations

The Precision Case Management Continuum

Back planning: each outcome listed above was to be built into one or more of clearly delineated case management stages that were sequenced as follows: Marketing Strategies - Worker Training - Eligibility – Orientation - Participatory Assessment (for Barriers and Vocational) - Career Counseling for the Local Labor Market - and Referrals (for vocational education or jobs). Each of these stages was to require specific worker checklists to ensure repeatability.

PCM Review

This PCM Review is conducted by the Director, DFA, to ensure identified PCM outcomes have been satisfactorily implemented within appropriate case management stages. Specifically, is each outcome adequately addressed in ways that are systemically applied using principals of visibility, repeatability and measurability to drive continuous process improvement through data.

TERRY SMITH

ABOUT THE AUTHOR

Terry Smith's first job was four years in the US Navy during Viet Nam. Later, he taught high school and college English before taking a master's degree in human services administration. He spent 26 years with New Hampshire's Health and Human Services directing poverty programs and is considered one of the nation's leading experts on welfare. He lives with his wife Elise amid thirty-eight acres of New Hampshire forest.

TERRY SMITH

ABOUT KHARIS PUBLISHING

Kharis Publishing is an independent publishing house with a core mission to publish impactful books, and channel proceeds into establishing mini-libraries or resource centers for orphanages in developing countries, so these kids will learn to read, dream, and grow. Every time you purchase a book from Kharis Publishing or partner as an author, you are helping give these kids an amazing opportunity to read, dream, and grow. Kharis Publishing is an imprint of Kharis Media LLC. Learn more at https://www.kharispublishing.com.